VITTORIO SERR

A DAY IN
FLORENCE

A New Practical Guide

152 colour illustrations
A map of the city
A compendium of useful hints

BONECHI EDIZIONI "IL TURISMO"

INDEX

ITINERARIES

FIRST ITINERARY

....

PIAZZA DEL DUOMO -BAPTISTERY -GIOTTO'S BELL TOWER
CATHEDRAL -CATHEDRAL MUSEUM
PALAZZO MEDICI-RICCARDI - SAN LORENZO
LAURENTIAN LIBRARY - MEDICI CHAPELS

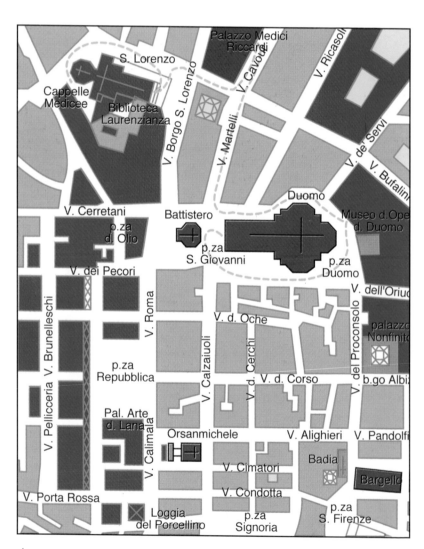

PIAZZA DEL DUOMO

Aerial view of Piazza del Duomo

At the dawn of the Middle Ages, the site of the Piazza was a mass of dwelling houses and public buildings. The church of Santa Reparata was built over the foundations of one of the latter in the 4th cent. Three centuries later, the Baptistery was built next to the church, and this area began to be the centre of religious life in Florence. Santa Reparata became a cathedral in 1128. The church was becoming too small for its new role and increased importance – the population was increasing too – and in 1289 the Commune decided to enlarge it. This was part of an extensive rebuilding project, involving new and more extensive city walls (the Roman circle was too small), the construction of a Priors' Palace (now Palazzo Vecchio) and alterations to existing buildings such as Santa Croce, the church of the Badia, Orsanmichele, the Bargello and the Baptistery. In order to achieve a city that should be new but harmonious, one man, Arnolfo di Cambio, was given the responsibility of directing and co-ordinating the work. One of the greatest architects and sculptors of his time, he raised the level of the piazza (which he had re-paved), eliminating the podium on which the Baptistery had previously stood, demolished a few houses nearby, and began to build the new cathedral, for which he planned a dome and external decoration matching that of the Baptistery. The death of Arnolfo in 1302 put a stop to the work, which was resumed in 1332-34 with the construction of the bell

tower under the direction of Giotto. The addition of a dome by Brunelleschi (1420-36) made it the impressive, dominating building that we see today (the façade dates from the 19th cent.).

BAPTISTERY

Dante's "Bel San Giovanni" (Fair St. John) the religious building most beloved by the Florentines, was perhaps started in the 7th cent., but the work done in the 11th and 12th centuries made it the most important monument of Romanesque architecture in Florence. Its regular octagonal form, the symmetrical distribution of the external decoration and the harmonic blending of marble were, for centuries, an architectural ideal for artists of the stature of Arnolfo, Giotto, Brunelleschi, Leon Battista Alberti, Leonardo and Michelangelo. It has three magnificent bronze doors. The **South Door** is by Andrea Pisano (*c.* 1330): it consists of 28 panels illustrating the *Life of the Baptist*; the bronze cornice is by Vittorio Ghiberti (son of Lorenzo, 1452). The **North Door** is by Lorenzo Ghiberti, cast between 1403 and 1424, after winning a competition in which Brunelleschi also took part; the 28 panels represent episodes from the *Life of Christ*. The East Door, the famous "**Door of Paradise**", is also by Lorenzo Ghiberti (1425-1452); it is composed of 10 gilded bronze panels, with complex *Scenes from the Old Testament* crowded with figures. The smooth pyramidal roof-covering is topped by a lantern. The **inside** of the Baptistery, like the outside, is on an octagonal plan with marble decoration and each wall divided into three by tall columns; the twin-arched windows of the women's gallery open above the trabeation. A *baptismal font*, mentioned by Dante in the Divine Comedy, used to stand in the centre of the fine inlaid marble floor but was removed in the 16th cent. by Buontalenti, by order of Grand Duke Francesco I. Against the wall are: a *baptismal font* of the Pisan school, 14th cent.; the *tomb of the anti-Pope John XXIII*, the work

Baptistry: *exterior;* below: *interior;* opposite: *aerial view of the Baptistry;* overleaf: *Door of Paradise,* by *Lorenzo Ghiberti*

Creation of Adam and Eve. -
Original sin. - Expulsion from
Paradise.

Story of Noah: Noah's family
leaves the ark after the Flood. -
Noah gives thanks to the Lord
who sends a rainbow as a sign of
peace. Drunkenness of Noah. -
Noah is derided by Ham and
covered up by Shem and Japhet.

Story of Jacob and Esau: Esau
trades his birthright for a plate
of lentils. - Isaac sends Esau
hunting. - Jacob throws a
goat-skin around his neck. -
Isaac mistakes Jacob for Esau
and gives him his blessing. -
Jacob leaves his father's house.

Story of Moses: Moses receives
the Tablets of the Law on
Mount Sinai. - Aaron waits
halfway down the mountain. -
The Hebrews, terrified by the
thunder and lightning, await
Moses' return at the foot of the
mountain.

Story of Saul and David: Saul
defeats the Philistines. - David
smites Goliath. -David carries
Goliath's head before the
cheering crowd, back to
Jerusalem.

Adam and Eve with their sons, Cain and Abel. - Man's first labour: Abel keeping sheep and Cain ploughing. - Cain kills Abel. Curse of Cain, the first act of justice.

Story of Abraham: Sarah at the entrance to the tent. - Apparition of the angels to Abraham. - Abraham and Isaac on the mountain. The Angel stays Abraham's hand as he is about to sacrifice Isaac.

Story of Joseph: Joseph is sold to the merchants and brought before Pharaoh. - Interpretation of Pharaoh's dream. - The golden cup in Benjamin's bag. - Joseph reveals himself to his brothers and forgives them. - Joseph meets Jacob.

Story of Joshua: Joshua and the Hebrews cross the Jordan, which recedes before the Ark. - The Hebrews gather twelve stones for commemoration. - The walls of Jericho fall at the sound of the Angels' seven trumpets.

King Solomon ceremoniously receives the Queen of Sheba in the Temple of Jerusalem.

Baptistry: *interior of the dome and the splendid mosaics;* below: *detail of Christ's face;* opposite: *South Door,* by *Andrea Pisano*

of Donatello and Michelozzo, commissioned by the banker Giovanni dei Medici; two Roman sarcophagi and a thirteenth-century altar. The beautiful and very striking wooden *statue of Mary Magdalene* by Donatello (1435-55), which used to be in the Baptistery, is now on view in the Cathedral Museum. The interior of the vault is covered by mosaics laid between the mid-13th and the mid-14th cent. by local and Venetian craftsmen (in the Middle Ages Venice was the greatest centre for mosaics). Among the most important artists who made the cartoons for the mosaics are Cimabue (*Scenes from the life of Joseph*) and Coppo di Marcovaldo (*Christ*). The subjects of the magnificent design are *Scenes from the Old and New Testaments* and the *Last Judgement*, dominated by the impressive figure of *Christ in Judgement.*

GIOTTO'S BELL TOWER

The building of this tower began in 1334 under the direction of Giotto, after a fire had destroyed the old bell tower of Santa Reparata. Giotto died in 1337, when the base of the tower had been completed; after him work was directed by Andrea Pisano and Francesco Talenti, who brought it to conclusion (although the original plan included a spire which was never built). The building is of remarkable grace and elegance; the structure lightens and lengthens as it rises, becoming complex with marble insets and fine tracery. The bas-reliefs on the base (the originals are in the Cathedral Museum) were carved by Andrea Pisano and his workmen under the supervision of Giotto.

Next to the bell tower, on the corner of Via Calzaioli, the graceful **Loggia del Bigallo**, built between 1852 and 1358 by Alberto Arnoldi, in elegant Gothic style, as a shelter for the town's waifs and orphans (Innocents). Its façade, facing the baptistery, has three tabernacles with the statues of *St. Peter Martyr, the Virgin and Child* and *St. Lucy*. Inside is a fine collection of works of art, with frescoes detached from the building and pieces by Ghirlandaio, Arnoldi and the schools of Botticelli and Verrocchio.

Giotto's Bell Tower and
the Loggia del Bigallo

View of the Cathedral; below: **Baptistry,** *South Door: detail of a bronze frieze,* by *V. Ghiberti*

CATHEDRAL

The construction of the Cathedral, dedicated to Santa Maria del Fiore (St. Mary of the Flower) was begun in 1294 by Arnolfo di Cambio, chosen by the city authorities and the citizens, who wanted a cathedral not only larger than the previous church of Santa Reparata but "so sumptuous and magnificent" that it would outshine the cathedrals of rival Tuscan cities both in beauty and dimensions. The new cathedral was constructed around the older church, the simple structure and two bell towers being incorporated. Santa Reparata was finally pulled down in 1375; but the Florentines went on calling the new cathedral by the old name for a long time - the authorities had to inflict heavy fines in order to enforce the use of the new one: "Santa Maria del Fiore". The lower part of Santa Reparata, buried underneath the floor of the Duomo till quite recently, can now be visited by going down a staircase from the right aisle; it contains remains of frescoes, sculptures and tombstones, that of Filippo Brunelleschi included. The stately and spacious interior

Cathedral: *interior*, below: *tombstones in Santa Reparata;*
opposite: *the façade*

of the Duomo was the scene of the fiery sermons of Savonarola and of the savage Pazzi conspiracy: on 26 April 1478 members of the Pazzi family, enemies of the Medicis, in league with Archbishop Salviati, attacked Lorenzo the Magnificent and his brother Giuliano during Mass. Lorenzo escaped, but Giuliano was killed and the conspiracy was followed by harsh repression. Works of art of many centuries embellish the cathedral but do not mask the severity of its high ogival arches and composite pillars. On the inside of the façade is an enormous clock, painted in 1443 and decorated with four heads of *Prophets* depicted by Paolo Uccello. Also by Paolo Uccello is the fresco of the *Monument to Giovanni Acuto* (John Hawkwood) on the wall in the left aisle; beside, left, is the *Monument to Niccolò da Tolentino*, by Andrea del Castagno (1456). Above the large octagonal tribune is the **dome** by Brunelleschi. A competition for the construction of the cupola was announced in 1418. The difficulty of this task was immediately evident, for traditional building techniques were inadequate. Brunelleschi invented an original system of mobile centres which superseded the usual one

Cathedral: *the choir;* below left: *Niccolò da Tolentino,* by *Andrea del Castagno;* below right: *John Hawkwood,* by *Paolo Uccello*

Cathedral: *inside the dome*

of fixed structures starting from the ground (clearly impossible to use owing to the enormous dimensions of the building) and so succeeded in defeating Lorenzo Ghiberti, his eternal rival, who also took part in the competition. The dome and the lantern were completed in 1436. The dome is based on a massive octagonal drum, has marble ribbing and is covered by red tiles baked in the kilns at Impruneta. The inside of the dome is decorated with frescoes by Giorgio Vasari and Federico Zuccari (1572-79) representing the *Last Judgement* in five superimposed bands. Over the high altar is a wooden *Crucifix* by Benedetto da Maiano and round it is the octagonal **choir** by Baccio Bandinelli (1555), decorated with bas-reliefs. Behind the altar on the right is the **Old Sacristy** with an *Ascension* in terracotta by Luca della Robbia in the lunette over the entrance. Directly opposite on the other side of the Tribune is the **New Sacristy**, with a fine bronze door by Luca della Robbia, Michelozzo and Maso di Bartolomeo (1445-69). In the lunette, *Resurrection*, also by Luca. Inside the sacristy, splendid fifteenth-century *inlaid cupboards*. In the chapel at the end of the apse is a bronze urn by Ghiberti with *relics of Saint Zanobius.*

The south-east side of Piazza del Duomo; below: *entrance to the museum*

CATHEDRAL MUSEUM

Situated behind the Cathedral, the museum contains works from the Cathedral, the Bell Tower and Baptistery. A room on the ground floor houses the sculptures from the original façade of the Cathedral, demolished in 1587, with a splendid *Virgin and Child* by Arnolfo di Cambio. The next room contains building material and mechanical devices used by Brunelleschi when building the dome. Another small room has a collection of precious reliquaries. The famous *Pietà* (Deposition) by Michelangelo is on the mezzanine. The seventy-eight year-old sculptor used a capital that came from an ancient Roman temple for this group, which he hoped would be his own grave monument in a chapel he owned in Santa Maria Maggiore in Rome. On the floor above: the two *choir balconies* by Donatello and Luca della Robbia; the Andrea Pisano marble *panels* from the bell tower; the statues of *the Baptist, Mary Magdalene* and *Habakkuk* by Donatello. Donatello's strongly re-

Left: *Pietà*, by *Michelangelo*; right: *Mary Magdalene*, by *Donatello*; below: *bust of Cosimo I dei Medici*, by *Giovanni dell'Opera*; bottom: *detail of the Choir*, by *Luca della Robbia*

alistic style in the statues of the prophets for the bell tower becomes astoundingly and exasperatedly tragic in his unique wooden Mary Magdalene. She is not the traditionally youthful beauty, which we find in most Florentine representations of the Saint, but a repentant old woman, a macabre and horrifying apparition of a being consumed by vice, sinful living and sufferings. See also the beautiful *silver altar* of the Baptistery, by Michelozzo, Pollaiolo, Verrocchio and others.

Turning right as we leave the museum, we walk back alongside the Cathedral and go right into **Via Martelli**. Lined with fine shops and important book stores, this is one of Florence's busiest thoroughfares. A short way up, in a little square on the left-hand side, we come to the **church of San Giovannino**, with its façade by Ammannati (16th cent.). Inside are frescoes and canvases by sixteenth- and seventeenth-century artists. Across the street is the huge, renowned Medici-Riccardi Palace.

19

Palazzo Medici-Riccardi: *the façade*

PALAZZO MEDICI-RICCARDI

B uilt for Cosimo the Elder between 1444 and 1460 by the Florentine architect and sculptor Michelozzo Michelozzi (a pupil of
Ghiberti who worked with Donatello), this was the prototype of
all Florentine palaces of the Renaissance. Majestic and elegant, it was
filled with works of art commissioned by the Medici. The main branch
of the family lived here until 1540. In 1655 the palace was sold to the
Riccardi family and is now the seat of the provincial administration and
the Prefecture. Exhibitions and other cultural events often take place
here. It was designed by Michelozzo as a large cube, and must have
stood out among the lower buildings round it, but the Riccardi family
had it enlarged, adding seven new windows. The two principal sides,
have pronounced rustication on the ground floor, flatter rustication on
the storey above and smooth stones on the third. This motif was to
reappear frequently for more than a century, along with the use of twin-
arched mullioned windows. There is a fine classical cornice, while the
big corner windows (called "kneeling windows" from the form of the
corbels) which replaced a previously existing loggia, are attributed to
Michelangelo (*c.*1517). On the same corner is a large Medici coat of
arms. Inside the palace is a fine porticoed **courtyard**, that contains Ro-

The Journey of the Three Kings to Bethlehem, by *Benozzo Gozzoli*

man remains and various pieces of sculpture. This palace used to contain many of the masterpieces that are now on view in the galleries and museums of Florence. One of the most important items is the **Chapel** by Michelozzo, at the top of the first staircase on the right from the courtyard. Here are the celebrated frescoes by Benozzo Gozzoli representing the *Journey of the Three Kings to Bethlehem* (1459-60) in which many personages of the time are portrayed: Lorenzo the Magnificent with his father, Piero the Gouty and his sisters; Galeazzo Maria Sforza; Sigismondo Malatesta; John VII Paleologus, Emperor of Constantinople; the painter himself and his master, Fra Angelico. There is also an interesting **Gallery**, reached by going up the second staircase on the right from the courtyard, decorated with stuccoes and mirrors at the end of the 18th cent., with a fine frescoed ceiling by Luca Giordano showing the *Apotheosis of the Medici Dynasty* (1682-83).

Outside the palace, the short **Via dei Gori**, flanking the building to one's right, leads into **Piazza San Lorenzo** – a picturesque and lively market square, dominated by the cumbersome bulk of the church of San Lorenzo with the Chapel of the Princes' dome behind it. The *monument to Giovanni dalle Bande Nere*, by Baccio Bandinelli (1540) stands at the Via dei Gori corner of the square.

Church of San Lorenzo: *the façade*

CHURCH OF SAN LORENZO

An ancient basilica, consecrated in 393 by St. Ambrose, bishop of Milan, it was probably the first church to be built on Florentine ground. Rebuilt in the 11th cent., it was radically restored in the 15th cent. for the Medicis, for whom it was the family church. The **interior**, spacious, light and elegant, is an early Florentine Renaissance masterpiece; it was designed by Brunelleschi in 1420 and he directed the work from 1442 until his death in 1446. It is in the form of a Latin cross and has a nave and two aisles with side chapels. There are numerous masterpieces, including two **bronze pulpits** by Donatello at the end of the nave, the master's last work (about 1460), completed after his death by pupils; a fine marble tabernacle by Desiderio da Settignano (mid 15th cent.) opposite the pulpit on the right; the *Marriage of the Virgin*, a painting by Rosso Fiorentino (1523) in the second chapel on the right; a remarkable *Annunciation*, with *Scenes of the life of St. Nicholas of Bari* by Filippo Lippi (*c.*1440) in the predella, in the left chapel of the left transept: also a large fresco representing the *Martyrdom of St. Laurence* by Bronzino (1565-69) in the left aisle opposite the pulpit. Finally, the **Old Sacristy**, exceptionally important for its architecture and works of art, is off the left transept. Elegant and of crystalline simplicity in its spatial conception, it fully expresses Brunelleschi's architectural ideal (1420-29). The eight fine tondi in the lunettes and pendentives (four with *Scenes from the Life of St. John the Evangelist* and four with the *Evangelists*) are by Donatello, as are the

Church of San Lorenzo: *the interior,* below: *the Cloister*

Laurentian Library: *Michelangelo's staircase, in the entrance vestibule*

two bronze doors beside the altar and a fine clay bust of *St. Laurence*; in the centre of the chapel, under a large marble table, is the tomb of *Giovanni di Bicci dei Medici* and *Piccarda Bueri*, the parents of Cosimo the Elder, by Andrea Cavalcanti (1434); on the left wall, under a large arch, is the tomb of *Piero the Gouty* and *Giovanni dei Medici*, sons of Cosimo the Elder, by Andrea del Verrocchio, helped probably by the youthful Leonardo (1472).

LAURENTIAN LIBRARY

The entrance is at No. 9, Piazza San Lorenzo, to the left of the church. Across the lovely, Brunelleschi-inspired **cloister**, the stairs in the right corner lead up to the Library commissioned by Clement VII in 1524, designed by Michelangelo and completed around 1578. It contains the magnificent collection of manuscripts, incunabula and codices amassed by Cosimo the Elder and the Magnificent Lorenzo such as the *Medici Virgil* (4th and 5th cent.), the *Pandects of Justinian* (6th cent.), the oldest existing examples of the tragedies of Aeschylus (11th cent.) as well as of the writings of Thucydides, Herodotus and Tacitus (tenth cent.). The building was begun by Michelangelo in 1524. The fine vestibule and the huge, elegant reading room are also his work.

Come out into the square and turn left alongside the church. The entrance to the Medici Chapels is in Piazza Madonna degli Aldobrandini.

Medici Chapels: *exterior*; below: *monument to Lorenzo, Duke of Urbino*, by *Michelangelo*

MEDICI CHAPELS

The memorial chapel mausoleum of the Medicis is an impressive architectural structure, appreciated for its statues by Michelangelo. Inside there is first a wide crypt, which leads up to the sumptuous **Princes' Chapel**, ordered by Ferdinando I in 1602. Work began two years later upon a plan by Matteo Nigetti, and Buontalenti, and continued for more than a century. The great octagonal space is lined with inlaid semi-precious stone wall panels of spectacular effect. Against the walls are the sarcophagi of six Medici grand dukes; above those of Ferdinando I and Cosimo II, statues in gilt bronze by Ferdinan-do Tacca; below: the sixteen coats of arms of Tuscan cities, in inlaid semi-precious stones. The chapel dome is frescoed with *Scenes from the Old and New Testaments*, by Pietro Benvenuti (1828). A corridor leads to the **New Sacristy**, the famous and beautiful chapel built by Michelangelo for Cardinal Giulio de' Medici, later Pope Clement VII. Michelangelo worked on it, through various vicissitudes, from 1520 until he departed from Florence for good (1534), leaving it unfinished. On a square plan, with its grey sand-stone (*pietra serena*) on white plaster, the chapel resembles the structure of Brunelleschi's Old Sacristy, but with much richer and more complex architectural decoration

25

Medici Chapels: *interior,* below: *the statue of Night on Giuliano's tomb,* by *Michelangelo*

(niches, windows, arches etc.). Out of the many tombs intended, the only completed ones are those of *Giuliano,* Duke of Nemours, and *Lorenzo,* Duke of Urbino, son of Piero the Unfortunate. The twin tombs are placed in the splendid architectural setting, with the marvellously idealised figures of the two men in Roman dress and armour sitting above the two sarcophagi, which are surmounted by the famous allegorical statues. Standing with one's back to the altar, *Giuliano's tomb* is on the left, (in reply to someone pointing out that the statue did not resemble the deceased man at all, Michelangelo was supposed to have retorted that nobody would notice that ten centuries on). Reclining figures of *Night* (a female figure sunk in sleep) and *Day* (a vigorous, muscular male figure in a rather strange and twisted position, the face incomplete) lie at each end of his sarcophagus. On the right, *Lorenzo,* wearing a helmet, sits nobly sunk in thought (he has in fact been nick-named "Il Pensieroso" or thinker). The reclining figures at his feet represent *Dawn* (a newly awakened girl - perhaps the finest and most famous statue of all) and *Dusk* (an old man, nodding wearily off to

Left: *Lorenzo's tomb*: right: *Giuliano's tomb*, below: *statue of Dawn*,
all by *Michelangelo*

sleep). Above the sarcophagus containing the remains of Lorenzo the Magnificent and his brother Giuliano, killed in the Pazzi conspiracy, is the beautiful *Virgin and Child*, also by Michelangelo, at which the two dukes contemplatively gaze; at the sides, *St. Cosmas* (left) by Montorsoli and *St. Damian* (right) by Raffaello da Montelupo, works by two pupils of Michelangelo that fall far below the expressive achievement of the statues near them. This work by Michelangelo, though unfinished, is generally interpreted as a lofty meditation on human destiny, its vanity and its redemption by religious faith. The three zones of the chapel can be understood in this sense: the lower order, with the tombs and allegorical statues, represents all-consuming Time that leads inexorably to death, to Hades; the middle band is the terrestrial sphere, and the upper one, more luminous, with the lunettes and the dome, the vault of Heaven. The sarcophagi seem rent in the centre by volutes surmounting the two urns, symbolically enabling the souls of the two dukes to flee the confines of space and time, to attain redemption in the domain of Eternity (the Virgin and Child).

SECOND ITINERARY

II

PIAZZA DEL DUOMO - CHURCH OF ORSANMICHELE
PIAZZA DELLA SIGNORIA -LOGGIA DEI LANZI
PALAZZO VECCHIO -UFFIZI GALLERY

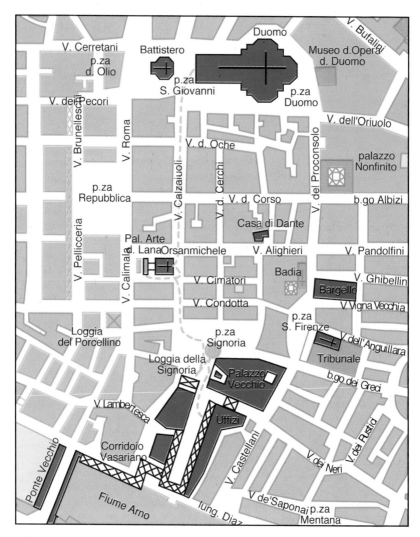

ORSANMICHELE

The religious and civic centres of Florence, Piazza del Duomo and Piazza della Signoria, are connected by **Via Calzaioli**, an elegant, busy shopping street, where the square bulk of Orsanmichele originally intended for secular use, was subsequently converted into a church. In 1284 the Florentine republic appointed Arnolfo to build a loggia for the collection and storage of grain, in the garden (*orto*) of the Monastery of San Michele – hence the name. This was burnt down in 1304, and rebuilt between 1337 and 1404 by Francesco Talenti and Neri di Fioravante in the slim, elegant, "decorated" Gothic style. The deposits were on the two upper floors, the grain flowed down to the loggia below through the chutes in the supporting pillars and out of the still visible openings. The external decoration was contracted out to the various city Guilds; each had a tabernacle with its coat of arms and the statue of its patron saint. Noteworthy, among the sculptures, are: the *Baptist* and *St. Matthew* by Ghiberti, *St. George* by Donatello (original in the Bargello) and the classical *Four Crowned Saints* by Nanni di Banco. The interior has a double nave with high cross vaults; in the right one, *tabernacle* by Andrea Orcagna (1359), a large Gothic cusped shrine, the base of which is decorated with bas-reliefs of *Scenes from the Life of the Virgin* and which contains Bernardo Daddi's panel of *Madonna of Mercies* (1347).

From top to bottom:
Coat of arms of the Wool Guild;
Via dei Calzaiuoli;
Church of Orsanmichele, interior

Orcagna's Tabernacle; below: *Palazzo dell'Arte della Lana*

Linked to Orsanmichele by a covered bridge, built to Cosimo I's orders, is the **Palazzo dell'Arte della Lana** (Wool Guild Hall), one of the most important guilds in Medieval Florence. Started in 1308 as the seat of the Corporation, it underwent various transformations over the centuries. In 1905 it was restored by Enrico Lusini and the fine frescoed rooms became the seat of the Dante Society. The fourteenth-century Gothic *Tabernacle of the Madonna of the Trumpet* on the corner of Via dell'Arte della Lana and Via Orsanmichele has a *Madonna* by Jacopo del Casentino.

Aerial view of Piazza della Signoria

PIAZZA DELLA SIGNORIA

Via Calzaioli ends in Piazza della Signoria. In Roman times, the area that is now the civic centre of the town was occupied by dwelling houses and the theatre. At the end of the 13th century, the area was included in the town-planning scheme directed by Arnolfo di Cambio, who requisitioned and pulled down the houses of Ghibelline families standing there and began to build Palazzo Vecchio. Henceforward the piazza became the setting for public speeches, ceremonies, meetings, uproars, executions: famous, especially, that of *Gerolamo Savonarola*, the preacher who was, for a short time, the arbiter of political life in the city and was excommunicated and burnt at

31

Piazza della Signoria with Sanonarola's martyrdom, in a late 15th-century painting; below: *Mercantile Tribunal*

the stake as a heretic on 23 May 1498, on the spot now indicated by a plaque in front of the Neptune Fountain. The Gothic Loggia was built in the 14th century. Opposite the latter, at N° 5, is the **Alberto della Ragione collection** (works of contemporary Italian art) and at N° 7 is **Palazzo Uguccioni**, built to a design by Michelangelo or Raphael, and on the east side the **Mercantile Tribunal**, built in 1359.

LOGGIA DEI LANZI

This is also called the Loggia della Signoria because it was built to shelter the public ceremonies of the Signoria, or even the Loggia dell'Orcagna from the name of the architect who, according to Vasari, designed it. The Lanzi were the Lanzichenecchi

Piazza della Signoria: *Loggia dei Lanzi*; below: **Palazzo Vecchio:** *Gothic pediment over the main door*

(L a n d - sknechts), G e r m a n mercenaries in the pay of Cosimo I, who used the Loggia as their bivouac for a certain period. The Loggia was built between 1376 and 1383 by Benci di Cione and Simone Talenti. It consists of three large classical round arches, supported by composite piers and a spacious cross-vaulted porch. The lobed panels between the arches were carved between 1384 and 1389 upon designs by Agnolo Gaddi and enclose statues of the *Virtues*. Two heraldic *lions* flank the entrance: the one on the right is an ancient Roman statue, the other is 16th cent. Under the right arch is the *Rape of the Sabines*, by Giambologna (1583), a work of refined virtuosity, which introduces the Baroque and was principally conceived to present and solve novel technical and compositional problems, wherefore it only received its name after it was finished. The left arch used to frame the *Perseus* by Benvenuto Cellini (1546-54), now removed to the Uffizi for restoration: the hero holding up the head of Medusa has a stateliness worthy of Michelangelo and

Rape of the Sabines, by *Giambologna*; right: **Perseus**, by *Benvenuto Cellini*
(in restoration at the Uffizi Gallery)

an almost Mannerist grace; the base is splendid, with statues and bas-reliefs that reveal the artist's skill as a goldsmith. The loggia also contains *Hercules and Nessus*, another group by Giambologna, *Menelaus Bearing the Body of Patroclus*, a Roman copy of a Greek original of the 4th cent. BC; six Roman female statues and the *Abduction of Polyxena*, a fine work by the nineteenth-century sculptor Pio Fedi.

NEPTUNE FOUNTAIN

Bartolomeo Ammannati was architect to Grand Duke Cosimo I. He contributed to restructuring Pitti Palace, rebuilding the Carraia and Santa Trinità bridges and he worked on numerous mansions all over Florence; as a sculptor, his most important work is this fountain in the piazza, commissioned by Cosimo and sculpted between 1563 and 1575. In the centre of the polygonal basin is the large

Piazza della Signoria: *Neptune Fountain,* by *Bartolomeo Ammannati*

figure of *Neptune* (whose bearded features recall the artist's patron, Cosimo), standing on a coach drawn by sea-horses; all round the edge of the basin, the magnificent bronze figures of *Naiads, Tritons* and *Satyrs* reveal the hand of Giambologna, Ammannati's assistant. On the steps of the Palace are placed: the *Marzocco*, the lion of the Florentine republic, a copy of Donatello's original, now in the Bargello; a copy of Michelangelo's *David*, now in the Academy, placed here in 1504 to personify the freedom that Florence yearned for in the brief republican period of those years; *Hercules and Cacus* by Bandinelli (1534) and two statuettes (perhaps *Philemon and Bausis* changed into plants) by De' Rossi and Bandinelli. On the left of the fountain is an imposing **equestrian monument to Cosimo I de' Medici** by Giambologna (1954). The reliefs around the base represent: the *Tuscan Senate Conferring the Title of Grand Duke on Cosimo I* (1537), *Pius V Presenting Cosimo with the Insignia of the Rank of Grand Duke* (1569), and *Cosimo Victoriously Entering Siena* (1557).

Palazzo Vecchio: *the façade*

Palazzo Vecchio: *the courtyard,* restructured by *Michelozzo;*
below: **the tower:** *detail of belfry*

PALAZZO VECCHIO

Palazzo della Signoria, called Palazzo Vecchio (the old palace) after the middle of the 16th cent. when the Medici left it and moved to Palazzo Pitti, has always been the seat of the city's highest political authorities (the Municipal Council still has its offices in the palace) and a symbol of the strength of established institutions. The building was begun in 1299 and was probably designed by the great architect Arnolfo di Cambio. The original edifice is a massive rusticated cube, three storeys high, with great twin-mullioned windows on the two main floors and a battlemented, covered and projecting passage-way supported on corbels, above which rises the handsome, mighty tower. Nine coats of arms symbolising the various regimes and rulers who have governed the Commune of Florence through the centuries are repeated in the arches formed by the corbels, see (for instance) the Florentine symbol of red lily on white ground. Trap doors in the floor of the passage were used to drop stones, boiling oil or molten lead on assailants, in the case of uprisings or attacks on the palace. The tower, 94 metres high, masterfully placed off-centre, was finished in 1310. The palace was repeatedly enlarged, in 1343, in 1495 (by Cronaca) and in the 16th cent. by Vasari (who considerably altered

37

Palazzo Vecchio: *Hall of the Five Hundred*; below left: *Victory,* by *Michelangelo*; below right: *Hercules and Diomedes*, by *Vincenzo de' Rossi*

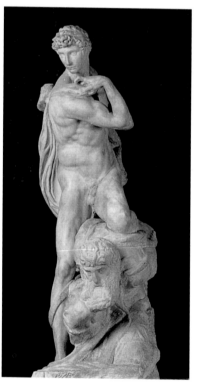

Palazzo Vecchio: *Study of Francesco I de' Medici*

the interior), by Giovanni Battista del Tasso and by Buontalenti. The interior of the palace is of the greatest interest both architecturally and because of its contents. On the ground floor, the fine **courtyard** by Michelozzo and the **Arms Hall** (entrance on the left side of the palace, used for temporary exhibitions); austere and bare, it is the only fourteenth-century room that has been left unaltered. On the first floor, the magnificent **Hall of the Five Hundred**, the **Hall of the Two Hundred** by the brothers Da Maiano (1472-77) with a fine coffered ceiling in wood (this housed the Council of two hundred citizens who discussed wars and alliances, and is now used by the Borough Council); the **Apartments of Leo X**, with a chapel and rooms frescoed with *Scenes from the Lives of the Medicis* by Vasari and helpers (only the rooms of Leo X, Lorenzo the Magnificent and Cosimo I can be visited because the others are occupied by the Mayor and aldermen's of-

Room of Leo X: below: *Florence during the Siege of 1530,* fresco by *Giorgio Vasari* (detail)

fices). On the second floor, the **Apartment of the Elements**, designed by Giovanni Battista del Tasso (*c.*1550). These rooms too were decorated by Vasari and helpers, some with fine inlaid cabinets. See also the lovely **Saturn Terrace** with its splendid view; the **Apartments of Eleonora of Toledo,** wife of Cosimo I, where special mention should be made of the **Gualdrada room**, with another fine ebony cabinet inlaid with semi-precious stones, and the **Chapel**, entirely frescoed by Bronzino, who also painted the very fine altar-piece (*Pietà*, 1553); the **Chapel of the Signoria**, the very fine **Audience Hall**, with coffered ceiling and marble doorway, both by Benedetto da Maiano, which contains a beautiful wooden bench designed by Vasari; the magnificent **Lily Room** with Donatello's famous, dramatic bronze group of *Judith and Holophernes* (*c.* 1455) and the **Map Room** and the **Chancery** next to it. Machiavelli, of whom there is a coloured clay bust and a portrait here, worked

Lily Room; below: ***Judith and Holophernes,*** by *Donatello*

in this room for several years as the Secretary of the Republic; and here is the original of the charming fountain in the courtyard, *Cupid with a Dolphin,* by Verrocchio (1476).

On the mezzanine (reached from the Hall of the Elements) is a series of fifteen rooms containing an important collection of works of art recovered in Germany after World War II. See for instance: the *Crouching Aphrodite,* Roman sculpture, 2nd cent. AD; two fine coloured panels in opus sectile, 331 AD; Greek and Roman reliefs and sculptures of various epochs. Among the Medieval and later styles exemplified here, note: a beautiful little painting on wood of the *Madonna of Humility* attributed to Masolino and another very small one attributed to Masaccio; a large *Nativity* by Antoniazzo Romano; *Pygmalion and Galathea* by Bronzino; a fragment, barely roughhewn but very fine, of the *Rondanini Pietà* by Michelangelo; *Venus and Mercury Present their Son Anteros to Jove,* by Paolo Veronese; *Leda and the Swan,* by Tintoretto; *Portrait of Elizabeth of*

Map Room

Valois, by Coelho; *Judith with Holophernes' head* and a large *Equestrian Portrait of Giovanni Carlo Doria* by Rubens; a beautiful *Portrait of an Unknown Man* by Hans Memling; the *Ecstasy of St. Cecilia* by Bernardo Cavallino; an exquisite *Portrait of Felicita Sartori* by Rosalba Carriera; Venetian landscapes attributed to Francesco Guardi and the circle of Canaletto; and a poignant *Maternity* by the nineteenth-century German painter Friedrich von Amerling. Also on the mezzanine are the **Museum of Musical Instruments**, containing rare and antique instruments of various periods, and the **Loeser Collection**, an important legacy of sculptures and paintings by Tuscan artists from the 14th to the 16th centuries. The most important pieces are: in sculpture, two terracotta groups representing soldiers and knights, by Giovan Francesco Rustici (16th cent.); a splendid *Madonna and Child*, in painted wood, attributed to the school of Arnolfo di Cambio and a marble *Angel* by Tino da Camaino; in painting: the *Passion of Christ*, a curious work by Piero di Cosimo, end of 15th cent.: "an abstract and original spirit", Vasari called him in his Lives; a *Virgin and Child* by Pietro Lorenzetti (first half of 14th cent.) and the remarkable *Portrait of Laura Battiferri* (wife of the sculptor Ammannati) by Agnolo Bronzino. A visit to the **tower** is recommended in order to enjoy a stupendous, sweeping panorama over the city and its surroundings.

View of the Uffizi Gallery

UFFIZI GALLERY

The Uffizi is not only the oldest art gallery in the world, it is the most important in Italy and also one of the greatest in Europe and in the whole world, visited by more than a million people every year. The gallery owns about 4800 works, of which about 2000 are on view (1000 paintings, 300 sculptures, 46 tapestries, 14 pieces of furniture and pottery, besides 700 more paintings kept in the Vasari corridor), the rest are in storage or on loan to other museums. This enormous quantity of works includes countless masterpieces, some being among the highest achievements of Western art. The building containing the Gallery was built for Cosimo I in the mid 16th cent. in the area between Palazzo Vecchio and the Arno to house the public offices (hence the name); the 11th-century church of San Pier Scheraggio, and the old Mint, where the famous Florentine florins were coined, were partly incorporated. The planning was entrusted to Giorgio Vasari (eminent and eclectic artistic figure of the time), who built it between 1559 and the year of his death (and that of Cosimo), 1574; the very original building, consists of two long porticoes joined by a third side that abuts on the Arno with a magnificent arch of great scenic effect. The outside of the Uffizi is inspired by the style of Michelangelo's vestibule for the Laurentian Library: grey *pietra serena* architectur-

View of the Uffizi Gallery overlooking the Arno

al elements against gleaming white plaster. Together with the marvellous Corridor, it is undoubtedly Vasari's architectural masterpiece. Work on the Uffizi was resumed in 1580 by order of Francesco I and directed by Bernardo Buontalenti, who built the large Medici Theatre (dismantled in 1890) and the famous Tribuna; at the same time the loggia on the top storey was rebuilt, the offices were transferred elsewhere and some of the rooms were used for collections of arts items, arms, and scientific curiosities, and so the Gallery was born. The first nucleus of works already included paintings by Botticelli, Lippi and Paolo Uccello; about 1600, Ferdinando I had all the works at the Villa Medici in Rome transferred to the Uffizi; in 1631 Ferdinando II contributed an important collection of paintings (originally in Urbino, the inheritance of his wife Vittoria della Rovere), including pieces by Piero della Francesca, Titian and Raphael; at the end of the 17th cent., Cosimo III collected gems, medals and coins and brought the *Venus*, later known as the "Medici" Venus, and other important antique sculptures; Anna Maria Luisa, Electress Palatine, the last heir to the Medicis, enlarged the collection with Flemish and German paintings and left it in its entirety to the state of Tuscany in her will (1743). In the 19th cent., after only part of the works of art stolen during the Napoleonic wars had been restored and after the creation of new specialised museums (Archaeological Museum, Bargello, Fra Angelico Museum, Museums of the Sciences, Silver Museum etc.) the Uffizi became what it is today.

View of the first corridor

Past the ticket counters, we enter the recently restored **church of San Pier Scheraggio** (within the building) traversing the gangway across the former crypt, on either side of which are Andrea del Castagno's renowned frescoed *Illustrious Men*. Originally painted for the Villa Pandolfini at Legnaia (15th cent.), they are representations of well-known literary and historical figures, from right to left: the *Cuman Sibyl, Boccaccio, Petrarch, Dante, Farinata degli Uberti, Pippo Spano, Queen Esther* and *Queen Tomiri*. The second hall, on the site of the church's apse, contains traces of the original decoration as well as works by fourteenth-century Tuscan painters. Sandro Botticelli's frescoed *Annunciation* graces the hall off to the right. The impressive staircase to the upper floors, designed by Vasari, is decorated with sculptures of various periods (some ancient), many of which are Roman copies of Greek originals. To the left of the second floor landing is the entrance to the **Gabinetto dei disegni e delle stampe** (Prints and Drawings Collection). This bountiful collection, started by Cardinal Leopoldo de' Medici, now comprises over 100,000 pieces by Italian and foreign artists.

The vestibule with antique statues on the second floor leads to the first wing of the picture gallery proper.

FIRST WING - The first gallery is the spacious loggia that Buontalenti restructured by order of Francesco I. On either side of the corridor are 4th to 6th century AD Roman sarcophagi, as well as Roman busts and statues. The ceiling decoration, in the so-called grotesque style, is by Allori and other sixteenth-century painters. The corridors are sometimes used to display some of the exquisite Flemish and Florentine tapestries in the Uffizi collection.

Left: *Virgin Enthroned with Angels*, by *Giotto*; right: *Rucellai Madonna*, by *Duccio di Buoninsegna*

ROOM I - (At the beginning of the corridor) Roman and Greek sculpture.

ROOM II - This is the hall of the thirteenth-century Italian school. The pieces displayed here give the observant spectator a splendid chance to perceive how and when Italian painting started to break away from the Byzantine tradition. The forerunners of what would be called the "Renaissance style" are Cimabue, here represented by a superb *Virgin Enthroned and Angels*, Duccio di Buoninsegna from Siena with his *Rucellai Madonna* (originally painted for the Rucellai Chapel in the Santa Maria Novella church), and perhaps the most revolutionary of all, Giotto, whose unique *Virgin Enthroned with Child and Angels* is opposite the entrance. Generally dated 1303-1305, when Giotto was reputedly working on the fresco cycle in Assisi, this painting's realism may be considered as the true beginnings of Italian painting. In addition, there are works by thirteenth-century artists from the school of Lucca: *St. Francis Receiving the Stigmata*, a triptych with the *Virgin and Child Surrounded by Saints*, and a *Crucifixion* from the school of Bonaventura Berlinghieri. Of note is *St. Luke the Evangelist* by the Magdalene Master, the *Saviour Amidst the Virgin and Saints* by Meliore di Jacopo, and a *Crucifix* with *Scenes of the Passion*, 12th-century Pisan school.

ROOM III - This room is filled with fourteenth-century Sienese art. They include major works by the Lorenzetti brothers: Ambrogio's *Presentation of Christ in the Temple* and the *Legend of St. Nicholas of Bari*, and Pietro's *Blessed Humility and SS. John, Mark, and Luke*. Perhaps the highlight amongst such treasures is an *Annunciation between SS Ansano and Judith* by Lippo Memmi and Simone Martini, a veritable masterpiece of lyrical grace and refinement. In addition, there is a *Virgin and Child* by Niccolò di Sozzo Tegliacci, a *Nativity* by Simone de' Cro-

Annunciation and Two Saints, by ***Lippo Memmi and Simone Martini;***
below: ***Descent from the Cross,*** by *Giottino*

cifissi, and a *Presentation in the Temple* by Niccolò Bonaccorsi.

ROOM IV - This room is dedicated to fourteenth-century Florentine painters, especially followers of Giotto. These include two *Virgin and Child with Saints* by Bernardo Daddi, Nardo di Cione's *Crucifixion*, Taddeo Gaddi's *Virgin in Glory*, and Giottino's *Descent form the Cross*.

ROOMS V-VI - The paintings here are typical examples of late four-teenth/early fifteenth-century Italian painting. This particular blend of Giotto-esque earthiness, Sienese refinement and great enthusiasm for elaborate ornamentation is known as International or "flowery" Gothic. Represented here are: Gentile da Fabriano (the lovely *Adoration of the Magi and Four Saints*) and Lorenzo Monaco (the huge *Coronation of the Virgin* and another *Adoration of the Magi*). Of note is the *Thebaid* attributed to Gherardo Starnina, whereas the three panels depicting *Scenes from the Life of St. Benedict* are by an unknown Northern Italian artist. In

Battle of San Romano by *Paolo Uccello;* below: *Adoration of the Magi,* by *Domenico Ghirlandaio*

addition there are Agnolo Gaddi's *Crucifixion,* and Giovanni di Paolo's *Virgin and Child with Saints.*

ROOM VII- Contains several masterpieces of fifteenth-century painting: *Coronation of the Virgin* and *Virgin and Child* by Fra' Angelico, *Virgin and Child Surrounded by Saints* by Domenico Veneziano, and the *Virgin with Child and St. Anne* by Masaccio and his teacher Masolino. A whole wall is taken up by Paolo Uccello's *Battle of San Romano* which once hung in Lorenzo the Magnificent's bedroom in the Medici-Riccardi Palace.

ROOM VIII - Fifteenth-century paintings, mostly by Fra Filippo Lippi (a predella strip of *S. Frediano Deviating the Serchio River;* the *Annunciation of the Death of the Virgin;* *St. Augustine in his Study;* the *Coronation of the Virgin,* which features fine portraits of several of Lippi's contemporaries; an altarpiece with the *Annunciation and Saints;* the charming *Virgin and Child and Two Angels;* an *Adoration of the Babe with St. Hilarion;* and another *Adoration with SS. John and Romuald*). Other painters represented are Alessio Baldovinetti (*Annunciation* and *Virgin and Child Surrounded by Saints*), the Sienese Lorenzo Vecchietta (*Virgin and Child Enthroned*), and Nicholas Froment (triptych depicting the *Resurrection of Lazarus*).

ROOM IX -The seated *Virtues* are by Antonio Pollaiolo, who, together with his brother Piero, painted the fine *Portrait of Galeazzo Sforza.* The *Portrait of a Youth with a Red Beret* is by Filippino Lippi, *Fortitude* by Botticelli and the *Adoration of the Magi* by Ghirlandaio.

Allegory of Spring and below: *The Birth of Venus,*
both by *Sandro Botticelli*

ROOMS X-XIV - This vast area is mostly devoted to works by the great master of delicate colour and soft, rhythmic line, Sandro Botticelli, whose cultured personality typified late fifteenth-century Florentine painting. The most famous are: the *Birth of Venus* and the *Allegory of Spring* (both masterpieces impregnated with symbolic meanings), grouped with the *Madonna del Magnificat*; the *Calumny*; the *Annunciation*; the *Adoration of the Magi* and the *Portrait of a Young Man with a Medallion*. The room also contains works by Roger Van der Weyden, Ghirlandaio and Filippino Lippi, and Hugo Van der Goes' superb *Portinari Triptych*.

Portinari Triptych: *The Adoration of the Shepherds,* by *Hugo Van der Goes*

Annunciation, by *Leonardo da Vinci*

ROOM XV - Contains two famous works by Leonardo da Vinci: the *Annunciation* and the *Adoration of the Magi*, as well as a remarkable *Pietà* by Perugino and a *Crucifixion* by Signorelli.

ROOM XVI - Known as the Map Room, frescoed with maps of Tuscany by Buonsignori.

ROOM XVII - This room is entered through the "Tribuna". Two important Hellenistic sculptures are here: *Amor and Psyche* and the famous *Sleeping Hermaphrodite* (2nd cent. BC).

Uffizi "Tribune", below: *Angel Musician,* by *Rosso Fiorentino*

ROOM XVIII - The "Tribuna" was designed by Buontalenti *c.* 1589 as a showcase for the Medici's most treasured pieces. Standing in the middle is the renowned *Medici Venus*, a Greek masterpiece of the 3rd cent. BC. The walls are hung with sixteenth-century portraits by various Mannerist painters: two female portraits by Bronzino are especially handsome – *Eleonora of Toledo* and *Lucrezia Panciatichi*. There are also fine paintings by Rosso Fiorentino, Vasari, and Carlo da Verona, not to mention the many pieces of Greek and Roman sculpture.

ROOM XIX - Dedicated to Signorelli and Perugino. Here are two of Luca Signorelli's finest paintings, the *Holy Family Tondo* and a *Virgin and Child.* There is also a lovely *Annunciation* by Melozzo da Forlì and items by two painters greatly influenced by Perugino, Lorenzo Costa and Gerolamo Genga. Perugino is represented by some portraits and the *Virgin between SS. John the Baptist and Sebastian.*

ROOM XX - Devoted to the German school, with paintings by one of the greatest, Albrecht Dürer: the *Calvary* (next to which is Brueghel's copy), portraits of *St. James the Greater and St. Philip the Apostle*, the *Adoration of the Magi, Portrait of the Artist's Father*, and a *Virgin and Child.* The portraits of *Luther and his Wife, Luther and Melanchthon,* and *Adam and Eve* are by Lucas Cranach. Other sixteenth-century German artists finish off the display.

Left: *Virgin Adoring the Child Jesus,* by *Correggio*; right: *Portrait of Benedetto di Tommaso Portinari,* by *Hans Memling*

ROOM XXI - Dedicated to fifteenth-century Venetian painting with an emphasis on Giorgione and Giovanni Bellini. The latter is represented by *Portrait of a Gentleman, Sacred Allegory* (the mysterious symbolism of which is immersed in a rarefied atmosphere), and the *Lamentation of Christ*. Giorgione's works are: *Moses before Pharaoh* and the *Judgement of Solomon*. Also: the *Halbardiers* and *Old Men*, by Carpaccio, *St. Louis of Toulouse* by Bartolomeo Vivarini, *Christ in the Temple* by Giovanni Mansueti, the delicate *Virgin and Child* by Cima da Conegliano, and *St. Dominic* by Cosmè Tura.

ROOM XXII - Paintings by German and Flemish Renaissance painters, including Hans Holbein, the great portrait painter (*Self-portrait* and *Portrait of Sir Richard Southwell*), Gerard David (the dramatic *Adoration of the Magi*), Lukas van Leyden (*Christ Crowned with Thorns*) and Albert Altdorfer (*Life of St. Florian*).

ROOM XXIII - Contains paintings by the Emilian Antonio Allegri, better known as Correggio (1489-1534), who was greatly influenced by Leonardo. Correggio's hallmark, soft colour, is evident in the works displayed here (the *Madonna in Glory*, the *Rest on the Flight to Egypt*, and the *Virgin Adoring the Child Jesus*). The *Adoration of the Shepherds* and the *Madonna of the Caves* by Andrea Mantegna are also here.

ROOM XXIV - Generally closed to the public, this room contains Italian and foreign miniatures from the 15th to 18th centuries.

SECOND WING -This section connects the two main corridors of the Uffizi. The works displayed are Roman sculptures. See: the *Boy Removing a*

Girl Preparing for the Dance, Roman copy of the original from 3rd cent. B.C;
right: ***Boy Removing a Thorn from his Foot**, Roman copy of the Greek original*

Thorn from his Foot, Venus, two *Roman Matrons,* and the delicate *Girl Preparing for the Dance.* From the great western window in the second (shorter) gallery, one enjoys a splendid view of the Ponte Vecchio with the **Vasari Corridor** running over it. Conceived as an aerial passage linking Palazzo Vecchio and the Uffizi to Palazzo Pitti, this singular feat of architecture and town planning was executed in the short space of five months, in 1565, by Giorgio Vasari, commissioned by Cosimo I. The Vasari Corridor starts from the Uffizi on the third floor between Room XV and Room XXXIV, runs along the Arno over an arcade, crosses the river over Ponte Vecchio, passes between houses and palaces on the other side of the river, traverses the façade of the church of Santa Felicita, continues along the side of Boboli Garden and, after a distance of nearly a kilometre, enters the Pitti Palace.

Used privately over the ages by the Grand Dukes, it was unfortunately damaged in World War II and only reopened in 1973; one has to book visits in groups. About seven hundred paintings are on view, including seventeenth- and eighteenth-century Italian works, **Portraits of the Medicis and the Hapsburg-Lorraines,** and above all the famous **Collection of Self-portraits,** the most complete in the world, extending from the 14th cent. to the present time, including nearly all the greater Italian artists and numerous foreign ones.

THIRD WING - This corridor too is decorated with some fine Roman sculptures, mainly dating from between the 2nd and the 4th cent. AD. At the beginning are two statues of *Marsyas before his Flaying* (the one on the right was retouched by Donatello). Farther on are a *Discus-thrower, Leda and the Swan,* and other Greek mythological figures.

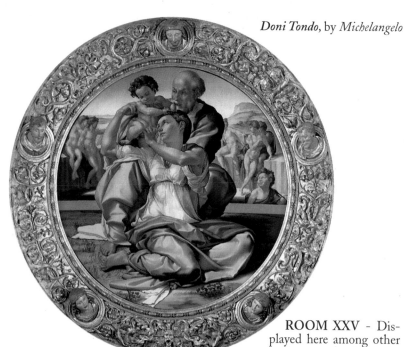

Doni Tondo, by *Michelangelo*

ROOM XXV - Displayed here among other masterpieces of sixteenth-century painting is one of Michelangelo's rare panel paintings, a *Holy Family* (the so-called Doni Tondo, commissioned by Angelo Doni). See also a *Portrait of Perugino*, attributed to Raphael, as well as works by Rosso Fiorentino and Mariotto Albertinelli, two Tuscan Mannerists.

ROOM XXVI - The Raphael room: the famous *Madonna of the Goldfinch, Leo X with Cardinals Giulio de' Medici and Luigi de' Rossi, Self-portrait* (on an easel), and *Portrait of Francesco Maria della Rovere* are all here. In addition, Andrea del Sarto, known as the "faultless" painter, a refined master of colour, is represented here by his masterpiece *Madonna of the Harpies*, not to mention fine pieces by Mannerists such as Pontormo (*Martyrdorm of St. Maurice*) and several portraits.

ROOM XXVII - This room is devoted to two refined sixteenth-century Mannerist painters, Bronzino and Pontormo. The *Holy Family, Lamentation of Christ,* and the exquisite composition of *Portrait of a Lady* are by the former, whereas the *Supper at Emmaus,* the *Birth of St. John the Baptist, Portrait of a Musician, Portrait of Maria Salviati,* and the *Virgin and Saints* were painted by Pontormo. There are also works by Franciabigio and Rosso Fiorentino.

ROOM XXVIII - This room is devoted to Titian (1477-1576) whose rich palette and emphatic use of light and shade became the hallmark of the Venetian school. Perhaps the best-known are the *Venus of Urbino,* the *Flora,* the portraits of *Eleonora Gonzaga* and *Francesca Maria della Rovere,* Duke and Duchess of Urbino, and *Venus and Cupid.* A fellow-townsman and follower of Titian's, Jacopo Palma, painted the *Resurrection of Lazarus,* the *Sacra Conversazione,* and *Judith.*

Madonna of the Harpies, by *Andrea del Sarto;* right: ***Madonna of the Goldfinch;*** below: *Self–portrait,* two of *Raphael's* works

ROOM XXIX - Several of Parmigianino's (1505-1540) finest works are hanging here: the *Virgin and Child with Saints,* a *Portrait of an Unknown Gentleman,* and the magnificent *Madonna dal Collo Lungo* (the Virgin with the Long Neck). Other artists represented are Ludovico Mazzolino, Luca Cambiaso, Scarsellino and Girolamo da Carpi.

ROOM XXX - The painters represented here belong to the Central Italian Emilia-Romagna school. Mazzolino is represented by the *Circumcision of Christ* and the *Virgin and St. Anne,* while Dosso Dossi by *Sojourn in Egypt.*

ROOM XXXI - Here are exhibited several works by Dosso Dossi: *Portrait of a Soldier,* the *Virgin in Glory,* and *Sorcery.* There are also paintings by sixteenth-century Venetians such as Lorenzo Lotto and Sebastiano del Piombo.

ROOM XXXII - This room contains works by a prominent Venetian artist Sebastiano del Piombo (1485-1547), known for his skill with luminous colour. A fine example is his masterpiece, the *Death of Adonis,* hanging here. In addition works by Lorenzo Lotto (*Sacra Conversazione, Susanna* and the *Elders*) and Paris Bordone (two portraits) are exhibited.

ROOM XXXIII - Also known as the "Sixteenth Century Hall" this passageway is hung with late sixteenth-century Italian and foreign works including François Clouet's *Portrait of Francis I, King of France,* Alessandro Allori's *Portrait of Torquato Tasso,* Bronzino's *Allegory of Happiness* and Jacopo Ligozzi's *Three Ages of Man.*

Venus of Urbino, by *Titian*

ROOM XXXIV - This room is devoted to Paolo Caliari, known as Veronese (1528-1588), one of the foremost sixteenth-century Venetian painters, appreciated for his uncluttered composition and colour shading. Displayed are his *St. Agatha Crowned by Angels*, the *Martyrdom of St. Justine*, the *Annunciation*, and the *Holy Family*. Other artists whose works hang here include Giulio Campi and Giovanni Battista Moroni, two prominent sixteenth-century portrait painters.

ROOM XXXV - Here one can admire important works by Jacopo Robusti, called Tintoretto (1518-1595) whose combination of startling light and shade contrasts intensely animated composition. The result is a uniquely dramatic effect that is typified in the *Good Samaritan*, the *Apparition of St. Augustine*, *Leda*, *Portrait of Jacopo Sansovino*, and *Portrait of a Red-haired Man*. The *Story of Joseph, Annunciation to the Shepherds,* and *Portrait of the Artist* are by another renowned sixteenth-century Venetian artist, Jacopo Bassani. In addition, there are works by Federico Barocci and El Greco.

From Room XXXV you go directly to Room XLI, as Rooms XXXVI to XL were eliminated when the Buontalenti Staircase was reopened after restoration.

ROOM XLI - Works by the Flemish masters Rubens and Van Dyck are here. Peter Paul Rubens' (1577-1640) impressive canvases of *Henry IV's Triumphal Entrance into Paris* and *Henry IV at the Battle of Ivry,* as well as two of his portraits - one of his wife *Isabel Brandt* and one of *Emperor Charles V*- offer splendid insight into the great Flemish painter's exuberant style. A few portraits by Anthony Van Dyck can be admired here, along with Justus Susterman's *Portrait of Galileo.*

ROOM XLII - This great room contains the statues of *Niobe* and of the *Niobedes*, Roman copies of 3rd to 2nd cent. BC Hellenistic originals, a

Noli me Tangere, by *Federico Barocci*

"*Medici*" Vase, neo-Attic (3rd-2nd cent. BC) and a *Rearing Horse*, Roman.

ROOM XLIII - The Caravaggio room houses the *Medusa, Bacchus* and the *Sacrifice of Isaac* by this great master of light and shade contrasts (1573-1610).

ROOM XLIV - Contains three magnificent works by Rembrandt (1606-1669): two *Self-portraits* and the *Old Rabbi*.

ROOM XLV - Among the paintings here are two charming *Views of Venice*, by Canaletto (1697-1768), a pair of *Capriccios* by Francesco Guardi (1712-1793) and two superb Goya *Portraits* (1746-1828).

THIRD ITINERARY

III

••

PIAZZA DELLA REPUBBLICA - STRAW MARKET
PONTE VECCHIO - PITTI PALACE -BOBOLI GARDENS
CHURCH OF SANTO SPIRITO
SANTA MARIA DEL CARMINE

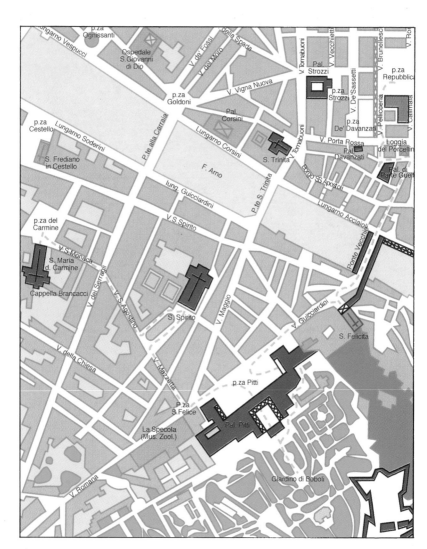

PIAZZA DELLA REPUBBLICA

In Roman times the city Forum stood where this piazza is today; there was a Temple of Jove and a column at the crossing of the two principal streets, *cardo* and *decamanus*, (respectively, the axis, Via degli Speziali -Via Strozzi, and Via Calimala -Via Roma). The Old Market, with its hovels, towers, loggias, stores and shops, all clustering round a column - known as the **Column in the Market** - on which was a *statue of Plenty*, replaced several times, superseded the Forum in medieval times. In the 19th cent., after an epidemic of cholera, the Commune decided to "wipe out centuries of squalor", as the plaque over the archway reads, and pulled down the whole complex, replacing it with the pompous architecture of today's square (at first named after Vittorio Emanuele II).

Top: *Piazza della Repubblica*; bottom: *Palagio dei Capitani di Parte Guelfa*

From Piazza della Repubblica along Via Pellicceria (the road with the porticoes) one gets to the **Palagio dei Capitani di Parte Guelfa** (the Palace of the Guelph Captains). The building stands in the small piazza of the same name, one of the most picturesque places in medieval Florence. Built in the 14th cent., it has a small, elegant façade with an outside staircase; it was enlarged in the 15th cent. (Brunelleschi contributed) and again by Vasari at the end of the 16th cent. The powerful judiciary that it housed was established in 1267, when the Guelphs defeated the Ghibellines. To the left of the Palace, Via Valdilamona leads to the

Straw Market, a picturesque, busy little market of articles of Florentine craftsmanship under the **Loggia del Mercato Nuovo** by Giovan Battista del Tasso (1547-51). The square-based loggia was ordered by Cosimo I for some of the most important corporations such as the bankers and the dealers in gold, wool and silk. Beside it is the entertaining *Boar Fountain* (Porcellino) by Pietro Tacca (1612).

Boar Fountain, bronze copy by *Pietro Tacca*; below: *Bust of Benvenuto Cellini*, by *Raffaello Romanelli*

To the left of **Via Por Santa Maria**, the road connecting the Straw Market to the Ponte Vecchio, is the ancient **Church of Santo Stefano al Ponte** in the little square named after the church, which has a simple Romanesque façade and a doorway decorated with marble in two colours (end of 13th cent.). The interior, with a single nave, was restored by Tacca in the 16th cent.; the structure of the unusual, highly elegant presbytery, preceded by a flight of steps by Buontalenti (1574) is flanked by a large altar on either side; there is a sixteenth-century choir with a coffered ceiling. On the third altar on the left is a bronze frontal with the *Martyrdom of St. Stephen*, by Tacca.

PONTE VECCHIO

As the name implies, it is the oldest bridge in Florence: it has, in fact, existed since the time of the Roman colony, when the piers were of stone and the roadway of wood; destroyed by flooding in 1117, it was completely rebuilt in stone but collapsed again in the terrible flood of 4 November 1333. It was rebuilt for the last time in 1345 (perhaps by the architect-cum-painter Taddeo Gaddi) with three spans, very wide, planned with room for shops on either side. First of all the butchers settled there (but later also grocers, smiths, shoemakers, etc.); these built the

Ponte Vecchio; below: *the bridge with its goldsmiths' shops*

typical shops with their back rooms projecting over the river, resting on supports and brackets. In 1591 Ferdinando I evicted them all, only allowing the shops to the goldsmiths; and since then the bridge has been like two long jewellery-shop windows, only interrupted by the two clearings in the middle, the one looking downstream has a *bust of Benvenuto Cellini*, "master of the goldsmiths" by Raffaello Romanelli (1900).

On the **Via Guicciardini** towards Piazza Pitti, we encounter the **Church of Santa Felicita** on our left in its little square, built on the site of an early Christian basilica of the 4th cent.; several times rebuilt, the last time by Ruggieri in the 17th cent. The Vasari Corridor runs across the top of the façade of the church. The Medici family and court used to walk from Palazzo Pitti to attend the religious services from within a balcony, without setting a foot out of doors. Inside, on the altar of the **Capponi Chapel** (first on the right) is a magnificent *Descent from the Cross* by Pontormo (*c.* 1528), a refined composition with fluid, translucent colours. On the right wall, there is an *Annunciation*, also by Pontormo. In the sacristy, we find a *polyptych* by Taddeo Gaddi. At the end of Via Guicciardini, the gigantic golden bulk of Palazzo Pitti stands out at the top of the slope to our left.

Palazzo Pitti; below: *the Pitti and the Boboli Gardens as they were depicted in 1599 in the lunette* by *Justus Utens*

PITTI PALACE

By the middle of the 15th cent., power was practically in the hands of the Medici family. Cosimo the Elder governed Florence from his new palace in Via Larga. Luca Pitti, however, his erstwhile friend, now led the faction that was most hostile to him and to his son Piero.

Luca, wanted a palace finer than the one that Michelozzo was building for the Medicis. He chose the site on the hill of Boboli and commissioned Brunelleschi to design a building with windows as large as the doorways of the Medici palace and so large, that the Medici palace would fit into his courtyard. Brunelleschi accepted with alacrity (Cosimo had previously rejected his plan for Via Larga) and produced the plans about 1445. Work began in 1457 (after the master's death) under the direction of Luca Fancelli, Brunelleschi's pupil. The façade overlooking the piazza consisted only of the seven central windows; it was on three storeys separated by slender balconies and covered with rusticated stone. At

The courtyard, built by *Bartolomeo Ammannati*

the death of Luca Pitti in 1473 the palace was still incomplete; then the Pitti family fell into disfavour, and Eleonora of Toledo, the wife of Cosimo I, bought the building and the land behind it in 1549. In the 16th and 17th cent. this became the palace of the Medici, who enlarged it, created a garden on the Boboli hill, lengthened the building to nine windows each side, employing Giulio and Alfonso Parigi, and decorated the interior sumptuously. In the 18th cent. Ruggieri and Poccianti built the two porticoed side wings that enclose the piazza (the so-called " rondò "). The remarkable fact is that each successive enlargement substantially respected the original design by Brunelleschi, both in form and material. During the period in which Florence was the capital of Italy (1865-71) the palace was the residence of Vittorio Emanuele II. Since 1919 it has been the property of the Italian State, together with its magnificent collections formed in centuries of devotion to art. There are seven museums here: the **Palatine Gallery**, the **Monumental Apartments**, the **Silver Museum**, the **Gallery of Modern Art**, the **Gallery of Costumes**, the **Coach Museum** and the **Porcelain Museum.**

The main doorway leads into the majestic Ammannati **courtyard** (1558-1570), a matchless scenario which is dominated by the *Artichoke Fountain* on the terrace above, on the garden side. Beneath the terrace are two smaller fountains dedicated to *Hercules* which flank the *Moses Grotto*, decorated with allegorical marble statues. The staircase on the right leads up to the first floor where one enters the Palatine Gallery.

Consequences of War, by *Pieter Paul Rubens*

THE PALATINE GALLERY

SALA DI VENERE (Venus Room) -The ceiling was frescoed by Pietro da Cortona and Ciro Ferri and adorned with exquisite stuccowork by Roman artists (1641-1642). Several extraordinary paintings are hanging here, including Titian's renowned "*La Bella*", probably a portrait of Duchess Eleonora Gonzaga from Urbino, a *Sacra Conversazione* by Bonifacio de' Pitati, a *Seascape* by Salvator Rosa, and *Portrait of Pietro Aretino*, one of Titian's late works. In addition, there is another Titian, a *Portrait of Julius II* which is a copy of a Raphael. Another Titian here, the *Concert*, once attributed to his master, Giorgione and now thought to be an early work painted by Titian while still in Giorgione's workshop. There are two Rubens: the *Peasants' Return from the Fields* and *Ulysses on the Isle of the Phaecians*. Francesco Bassano painted the *Martyrdom of St. Catherine* and Guercino *Apollo and Marsyas.*

SALA DI APOLLO (Apollo Room) -The ceiling fresco is by Pietro da Cortona and Ciro Ferri (1647-1660). The series of great Titians continues here with the *Magdalen* and his very famous *Portrait of the Grey-Eyed Youth*, a work of mysterious charm. In addition, there is a superb Tintoretto, *Portrait of Vincenzo Zeno*, as well as *Nymph Chased by a Satyr* and *St. John the Baptist* by Dosso Dossi, the *Holy Family* and a magnificent *Deposition*, by Andrea del Sarto, a splendid altarpiece by the Mannerist painter Rosso Fiorentino of the *Virgin and Saints*, a fine *Self-portrait* by Andrea del Sarto, and lastly a double portrait by Anthony Van Dyck, *Charles I of England* and *Henrietta Maria* his French Bourbon queen.

SALA DI MARTE (Mars Room) -The ceiling fresco of *Mars and Hercules* was again painted by Pietro da Cortona and Ciro Ferri (1643-45). In addition to two charming versions of the *Virgin and Child* by the Spanish artist, Murillo, there are two major Rubens: a portrait group entitled the *Four Philosophers* (the first

Left: *Magdalen*, by *Titian*; right: *La Velata*, by *Raphael*;
below: *Victory*, marble statue by *V. Consani*

standing figure on the left is a self-portrait) and the renowned *Consequences of War*, a huge canvas painted by Rubens in Antwerp in 1638. Commissioned by Ferdinando II, the subject was inspired by the bloody Thirty Years' War. Two fine Titian portraits: *Ippolito de' Medici* and *Andrea Vesalio*, Van Dyck's *Portrait of Cardinal Bentivoglio* considered one of his finest, Tintoretto's *Portrait of Luigi Cornaro,* and Veronese's *Portrait of Daniele Barbaro*. Also works by Guido Reni and Guercino.

SALA DI GIOVE (Jupiter Room) -The mythological scenes on the ceiling are by Pietro da Cortona and Ferri (1643-1645). In the middle of the room is a marble statue of *Victory* by Vincenzo Consani (1867). One of Raphael's best-known paintings, *La Velata* (Lady with a Veil), is here. The model who sat for the portrait was probably Raphael's mistress, la Fornarina (the baker girl), who often served as his model. Other fine paintings in the room: Borgognone's *Battle Scene*, Andrea del Sarto's, *Portrait of the Artist and his Wife* and his charming *Annunciation*, Bronzino's *Portrait of Guidobaldo della Rovere*, Rubens' *Nymphs Chased by Satyrs*, and Fra Bartolomeo's striking *Deposition*.

SALA DI SATURNO (Saturn Room) -The ceiling fresco by Ferri (1663-1665) is based upon a design by Pietro da Cortona. This room contains a number of Raphael's major works, including the much loved *Madonna of the Chair*, where the figures' full, rounded forms belong to the artist's Roman period; the *Portrait of Cardinal Dovizi da*

Bibbiena; the unfinished *Madonna del "Baldacchino"* (Virgin of the Canopy); and the *Wedding Portraits of Agnolo and Maddalena Doni*. Also the famous *Madonna del Granduca* of 1505. A subtle blend of Leonardesque and Umbrian influence (Raphaels' early style as he grew up in Umbria where he studied under Perugino). Also here: Perugino's *Deposition*, painted in Florence in 1495 and the *Magdalen*, with intense light and shade contrasts. Also: Ridolfo del Ghirlandaio's *Portrait of a Goldsmith*.

SALA DELL'ILIADE (Iliad Room) -The ceiling decoration by Luigi Sabatelli portrays *episodes from Homer's Iliad*. The statue in the middle by Lorenzo Bartolini (1824) represents *Charity*. The highlights of the room are Velasquez's *Portrait of Philip IV of Spain*, a series of end of the 16th- and beginning of the 17th-century portraits, by Justus Sustermans - official portrait painter to the Medici court at the time, among which his masterpiece, a portrait of *Count Valdemar, Christian of Denmark*. Also a *Portrait of King Philip II of Spain* by Titian, two *Assumptions* by Andrea del Sarto and Raphael's *Portrait of a Lady* known as "La Gravida" (the pregnant woman).

SALA DELL'EDUCAZIONE DI GIOVE -(Room of the Education of Jupiter - to the right of the Sala dell'Iliade). The room was named after the mythological scene of the ceiling fresco by Luigi Catani (1819). The paintings displayed are a striking *Portrait of a Man* by Van Dyck, Caravaggio's famous *Sleeping Cupid*, a *Pietà* by Francesco Salviati, and the *Chaste Susanna* by Guercino. The head of Holofernes in Cristoforo Allori's *Judith* is supposedly a self-portrait of the artist.

SALA DELLA STUFA (Room of the Stove) -The walls and ceiling of this room are entirely frescoed by Matteo Rosselli and Pietro da Cortona.

SALETTA DA BAGNO (Bathroom) -The neo-classical decorative scheme of stuccowork and bas-reliefs is by Giuseppe Cacialli.

SALA DI ULISSE (Ulysses Room) -The rather mediocre ceiling fresco by Gaspare Martellini, depicting *Ulysses' Return to Ithaca*, was meant to symbolise Ferdinando III's return to Florence after Napoleon's defeat. There are several paintings by Carlo Dolci (the *Virgin and Child* is especially charming). Cigoli's *Ecce Homo*, Tintoretto's *Portrait of Andrea Frazier*, Filippino Lippi's *Death of Lucretia*, Raphael's *Madonna dell'Impannata* ("impannata" indicates the oiled cloth on the window) and a *Portrait of Alfonso di Ferrara* attributed to Titian.

SALA DI PROMETEO (Prometheus Room) -The frescoed ceiling and walls, by Giuseppe Collignon (1842), depict *Scenes from the Myth of*

Left: *La Gravida,* and right: *Madonna dell'Impannata,* by *Raphael;* below: *the Beautiful Simonetta,* by *Botticelli;* opposite: *Madonna of the Chair,* by *Raphael*

Prometheus. The paintings in the room include Pontormo's *Eleven Thousand Martyrs*, Mariotto Albertinelli's *Holy Family* and Luca Signorelli's treatment of the same subject, Filippo Lippi's charming tondo of the *Virgin and Child* and Francesco Botticini's *Virgin and Child with Angels.*

POCCETTI GALLERY - The ceiling was frescoed by Bernardo Poccetti (16th cent.). There are two *portraits* by Rubens, *Ila and the Nymphs* by Francesco Furini, the *Martyrdom of St. Bartholomew* by José de Ribera (Lo Spagnoletto), four *landscapes* by Poussin, and the *Missing Drachma* by Domenico Fetti.

SALA DELLA MUSICA (Music Room) -It is also known as the Drum Room from the drum-shaped furniture. The *table* in the middle is made of Russian malachite and has gilded bronze supports.

SALA CASTAGNOLI - The room was named after the painter who decorated it in the 19th cent. The round table in the middle is inlaid with precious stones. Made in Florence in 1851 and known as the *Table of the Muses,* it shows *Apollo in his Chariot* surrounded by *Symbols of Muses.* The bronze support with *Seasons* and *Cupids* is by Giovanni Duprè (19th cent.).

SALA DELLE TRE ALLEGORIE (Allegory Room) -The room is also known as "Sala

Wedding Night, by *Giovanni da San Giovanni*; below: ***Sala delle Allegorie***

del Volterrano" (Volterrano was called the painter - real name Baldassare Franceschini - who frescoed the allegorical scenes). The paintings include the *Pranks of Pievano Arlotto, Profane Venus*, and *Sleeping Cupid*, all by Volterrano, the *Virgin and Child* by Artemisia Gentileschi, as well as *Venus and Amor* and the *Wedding Night* by Giovanni da San Giovanni.

SALA DELLE BELLE ARTI (Art Room) - Frescoed by Podestà (19th cent.). Paintings by Dolci, Ligozzi, and Rustici, and an *Adoration of the Magi* by Cristoforo Allori.

SALA DELL' ARCA (Ark Room) - Frescoed in 1816 by Luigi Ademollo to represent the pavilion David built for the Ark.

CAPPELLA DELLE GRAN-DUCHESSE or DELLE RELIQUIE (the Chapel of the Grand Duchesses, also known as the Reliquary Chapel) Decorated with gilded stuccowork and frescoes in the early 17th cent. for Maria Magdalena of Austria as a private chapel for the grand duchesses.

The previous room gives onto a narrow one containing small paintings of the Flemish, German and Florentine schools. Of note are the works by Paul Brill and Van Mieris and some splendid miniatures of fruit by Giovanna Garzoni (17th cent.).

Throne Room

THE MONUMENTAL or EX-ROYAL APARTMENTS - These magnificent apartments were the living quarters of the Medici, the Hapsburg Grand Dukes and, in the 19th cent., of the Italian sovereigns, the Savoy family.

The first room with portraits of the Medici family by the court painter Sustermans, is also called the SALA DELLE NICCHIE (Niches Room). Sèvre and Japanese vases are placed in the corners.

SALA VERDE (Green room) - is hung with Gobelins tapestries. The allegorical frescoes honouring the Medici are by Luca Giordano.

SALA DEL TRONO (Throne Room) - was where the kings of Italy took oath. The room contains portraits by Sustermans and Francesco Porbus, as well as magnificent majolica vases.

SALA CELESTE (Blue Room) - is decorated with Gobelins tapestries, portraits by Sustermans and rare Chinese vases.

The CHAPEL with portraits of Medici Cardinals by Sustermans.

SALA DEI PAPPAGALLI (Parrot Room) was named for the "parrot" (actually eagle) motifs in the Empire-style tapestries. There are paintings by Titian (*Portrait of the Duchess of Urbino*) and Hans von Aachen (*Portrait of Francesco I).* This room and the following two were Queen Margherita's Suite. The SALA GIALLA (Yellow Room), is hung with Gobelin tapestries, as well as portraits, one, attributed to J.F. Douven, depicts the *Electress Palatine*. The queen's bedroom contains some fine Empire furniture.

Brunelleschi Tries Out the Egg Tempera, by *Giovanni Fattori;*
below: *semi-precious stone vases,* from the Medici Collection

Back in the Sala dei Pappagalli, we enter King Umberto I's suite. The bed-room, study, and living room are decorated with tapestries and portraits. The SALA DI BONA was frescoed by Poccetti with scenes showing the *Conquest of the City of Bona in Africa,* the *Conquest of Prevesa,* a *View of Leghorn Harbour* and an *Apotheosis of Cosimo I.*

SALA BIANCA (White Room), the ballroom's ceiling and walls are covered with Neo-classical stuccoes. Beautiful chandeliers hang here. Used by the Hapsburgs and the Savoy sovereigns for official receptions.

After viewing the Palatine Gallery and the Royal Apartments, we go up to the second floor of the palace and enter the Gallery of Modern Art.

GALLERY OF MODERN ART - Founded by the Tuscan provisional government in 1860, this museum contains a fascinating Italian nineteenth-century collection. In addition to the neo-classical and academic schools profusely represented, there are also numerous paintings belonging to a Tuscan movement called "I Macchiaioli" (from "macchia" = splash or mark) which was akin and contemporary with (but not influenced by) the French Impressionist Movement. The "Macchiaioli" artists strove to free themselves from the restrictions and conventions of academic art, seeking inspiration in nature and reality.

Left: *The Cock;* right: *The Fisherman,* the Electress Palatine's
jewellery collection

Works by Giovanni Fattori, the head of the movement, and of all its major exponents may be viewed. There are also works by living contemporary artists.

SILVER MUSEUM - Instituted in 1919 on the ground floor of Pitti Palace, in the rooms that were used as the summer apartments of the Grand Dukes. Among the most interesting of these, from the point of view of decoration, are the Room of Giovanni da San Giovanni and the three successive ones, frescoed by Colonna and Mitelli between 1638 and 1644. The prestigious collection includes goldsmiths' work, enamels, cameos, crystal and carved or inlaid semi-precious stone objects, acquired by the Medicis and the Hapsburgs. Among the most important pieces are: semi-precious stone vases belonging to Lorenzo the Magnificent; seventeenth-century German ivories; a *vase in lapis lazuli* by Buontalenti (1583): the jewels of the bishop-princes of Salzburg; a *drinking cup belonging to Diane de Poitiers* (16th cent.); a relief in gold, enamel and semi-precious stones of *Cosimo II in Prayer* (17th cent.).

COACH MUSEUM -(The entrance is under the arcade of the right wing of the palace). This fascinating little museum contains the carriages in use from the 16th to the 19th centuries, as well as fittings and costumes dating from various periods. In the entrance hall are precious fittings that once belonged to the Medici and the Savoy families. In addition, prints showing costumes of the Medici court in the 18th cent. The second room contains the exhibition of coaches, among which: the *sedan* belonging to the *Electress Palatine Maria Luisa* (18th cent.) the *coaches* belonging to the *Duke of Modena, Francesco II* (1500), to the *Grand Duke of Tuscany, Leopoldo II* (1815), to the *King of Naples, Ferdinando II* (1839) and *Catherine de Médicis,* as well as the special *chair Grand Duke Cosimo II* used for going up and down stairs, after he became lame.

Back in the square, one goes into the Boboli Gardens through the left wing gateway.

Palazzo Pitti viewed from the Boboli Gardens

BOBOLI GARDENS

The gardens were laid out on the Boboli hill shortly after Pitti Palace became the property of Cosimo I and Eleonora of Toledo, towards the second half of the 16th cent. The architect and sculptor Niccolò Pericoli, called "Tribolo", was given the task of designing a garden in accordance with the new Renaissance mode which exacted more stately proportions than the Medieval private "viridarium" (or greenery) had accustomed people to. The Renaissance garden was the symbol of the Prince's power, the scene of parties and plays, a place of relaxation for the court, where one could wander through groves populated by allegorical statues, grottoes and fountains. Boboli underwent many alterations owing to variations in taste, but the design remained substantially the same. Near the entrance is the curious *Bacchus Fountain* in which Valerio Cioli portrayed a dwarf of the court of Cosimo I astride a tortoise. Further on is the *Grotto by Buontalenti*, built between 1583 and 1588 for the eccentric Francesco I; the first chamber is like a real cave decorated with sculptured forms that look like animals. In the corners are four copies of Michelangelo's *Prisoners* (Accademia Gallery) - the originals used to stand here. In the cave behind, the group of *Paris and Helena*, by Vincenzo de' Rossi. Last comes a small grotto with a *Venus* by Giambologna. Going on, one comes to

Oceanus Fountain, by *Giambologna;*
below: *Bacchus Fountain,* by *Valerio Cioli*

the *Amphitheatre*, first made in grass in the 16th cent. and remade in the 18th, for the performance of plays. The Egyptian obelisk in the centre was brought to Rome from Luxor in the Imperial epoch. Going up to the left one comes to the *Neptune* *Fishpond* and the *Giardino del Cavaliere*, where the **Porcelain Museum** is; or going straight on, along a wide *avenue*, one reaches the beautiful *Piazzale dell'Isolotto*, with its large pool and island, planted with lemon trees, and the *Oceanus Fountain* by Giambologna.

From Piazza Pitti, one crosses Piazza San Felice and turns right into Via Mazzetta which leads to the very attractive **Piazza Santo Spirito**. Number 10 is **Palazzo Guadagni,** an outstanding Florentine Renaissance palace, attributed to Cronaca (1503-1506). The building has two orders of arched windows, is crowned by a graceful loggia and sports a lovely wrought-iron lantern on the corner.

Piazza Santo Spirito

SANTO SPIRITO

The church of Santo Spirito stands on the northern side of the square. The original plan, by Filippo Brunelleschi (1444), was for a church facing in the opposite direction, towards the Arno, overlooking a large piazza; but it could not be carried out owing to the opposition of the landowners involved. After Brunelleschi's death, his design was largely respected by Antonio Manetti and other pupils as regards the interior, while the simple façade is 17th cent. The slender **bell tower** was built by Baccio d'Agnolo at the beginning of the 16th cent. The spacious and solemn **interior** recalls the symmetry and rhythmical perfection achieved by Brunelleschi in San Lorenzo, except for the variation of a dome above the presbytery and the continuation of the side aisles in the transept and the apse. The elaborate Baroque high altar by Giovanni Caccini (1608) stands in the centre of the presbytery. In the right transept is a fine *Virgin and Child with Saints and Patrons* by Filippino Lippi (*c.*1490) with an interesting view of Florence in the background. In the apse is a polyptych by Maso di Banco representing the *Virgin and Child with Saints*; on a nearby altar is a painting of the *Holy Martyrs* by Alessandro Allori (1574). In the predella is a view of the original façade of Pitti Palace. In the left transept is the **Corbinelli Chapel**, an elegant piece of architecture and sculpture by Andrea Sansovino (1492). Next to it is the *Holy Trinity with SS. Catherine and Magdalene* attributed to Francesco Granacci. Off the left aisle is an elegant vestibule by Cronaca (1494) with a fine barrel vault. This leads into the beautiful octagonal **Sacristy**, with dome, by Giuliano da Sangallo (1492). Leaving

Santo Spirito: *interior,* right: *Holy Trinity with SS. Catherine and Magdalene,* attributed to *Francesco Granacci* (detail)

the church, on the right is the entrance to the **Cenacolo**, the refectory of the Augustinian monastery that used to exist here. The wall at the end of the room is covered with a large fresco by Andrea Orcagna (*c.*1360) representing two scenes, one above the other: a wonderful *Crucifixion* and a *Last Supper* (now in very poor condition).

Crossing the square, we turn right into Via Sant'Agostino, go over Via de' Serragli, and continue down Via Santa Monaca until we come to **Piazza del Carmine.**

SANTA MARIA DEL CARMINE

With Santo Spirito, this is the most important church on the south side of the Arno. It was founded in 1268 by the Carmelite Friars. In 1771 it was burnt down, except for the Corsini and Brancacci chapels and the sacristy; however, the parts destroyed were completely rebuilt a few years later. The unfinished façade is a high, severe wall of rough stone. The **interior** is prevalently 18th cent. The **Corsini Chapel**, at the end of the left transept, by Silvani and Foggini, with ceiling frescoed by Luca Giordano with the *Apotheosis of St. Andrea Corsini* (1682), is a seventeenth-century masterpiece. At the end of the opposite transept is the main feature of the church: the

Church of Santa Maria del Carmine

Brancacci Chapel, the decoration of which is a milestone in Western art history. The murals were commissioned in 1425 by Felice Brancacci, a rich Florentine merchant and diplomat, from the painter, Masolino da Panicale, who still conformed to the Gothic taste, but was also open to the new ideas that were beginning to emerge in Tuscan painting at the time - and the pioneer, the great master of this renewal, was the colleague Masolino chose to work with him on the Brancacci Chapel: Masaccio. The latter probably took the older painter's place in the following year, when Masolino was called to the court of Hungary, but for reasons unknown (perhaps his extreme poverty obliged him to leave the city), he did not finish the work, which was completed by Filippino Lippi between 1481 and 1485. The best of Masaccio's brief career (he died in 1428 at the age of 27) is in the Brancacci Chapel: his frescoes won the unconditioned admiration of Verrocchio, Fra Angelico, Leonardo, Botticelli, Perugino, Michelangelo and Raphael: his startling rediscovery of the classical laws of perspective which, for the first time in Italian painting, endows his figures with an almost sculptural solidity, the dramatically essential way in which he relates the episodes of the New and Old Testaments, recalls the superb simplicity of Giotto, but also make him the first great master of the Italian Renaissance. The cycles of illustrations on the walls of the Brancacci Chapel are two: *Original Sin* and *Scenes from the Life of St. Peter;* among the most significant are the *Expulsion from Paradise*, a powerful masterpiece by Masaccio which faces the quite different dramatic tension in the *Temptation of Adam and Eve* by Masolino, on the wall opposite; *St Peter Heals a Cripple and Restores Tabitha to Life,* by both artists; *St. Peter baptising the Neophytes* by Masaccio; *The Tribute Money,* also by Masaccio.

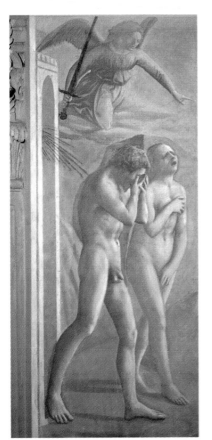

Left: *Expulsion from Paradise,* by *Masaccio*; right: *Temptation of Adam and Eve,* by *Masolino*; below: *The Tribute Money,* by *Masaccio*

FOURTH ITINERARY

PIAZZA DEL DUOMO -VIA TORNABUONI
STROZZI PALACE - SANTA TRINITA
PALAZZO DAVANZATI - SANTA MARIA NOVELLA

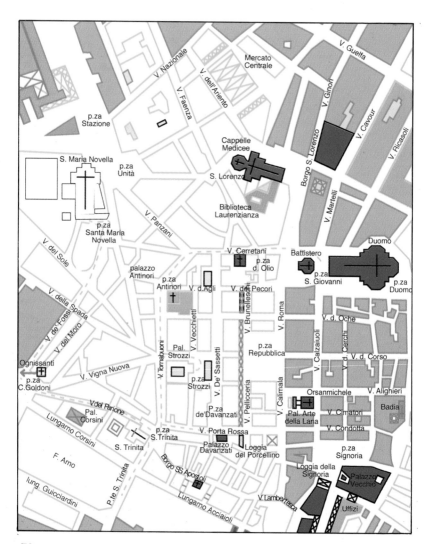

Via dei Cerretani - One of the busiest thoroughfares in the city, this street goes from Piazza del Duomo to the central railway station. A few yards down on the left, it passes the **Church of Santa Maria Maggiore**. First built in the tenth cent. within the old city walls, it was later rebuilt at the end of the 1200s. Over the portal is a sculpture of the *Virgin and Child* (14th-cent. Pisan school). Inside the Gothic interior is the *tomb of Brunetto Latini*, Dante's master. In the chapel to the left of the choir is a thirteenth-century painted relief of the *Virgin Enthroned with Child* attributed to Coppo di Marcovaldo.

Via Tornabuoni

- Continuing down Via dei Cerretani, we soon turn left into Via Rondinelli, in turn leading into **Piazza Antinori**. The square is named for the elegant fifteenth-century **Palazzo degli Antinori** on the right, attributed to Giuliano da Maiano. Opposite the palace is the **Church of San Gaetano**. Originally a Romanesque structure, it was entirely rebuilt in the Florentine Baroque style by Matteo Nigetti, Gherardo and Pier Francesco Silvani in 1648. The aisleless interior is lined in black marble. In the second chapel on the left is the *Martyrdom of St. Laurence* painted by Pietro da Cortona.

Via Tornabuoni - This is Florence's most aristocratic street, indeed one of the most beautiful in the world. Lining it are lovely old mansions with elegant shops. On the right at Number 19 is **Palazzo Larderel,** a lovely late Renaissance building designed by Giovanni Antonio Dosio (1580). Opposite, at number 20, is **Palazzo Corsi.** It was restructured in 1875, although the original construction was designed by Michelozzo whose elegant inner courtyard is still extant. **Palazzo Viviani,** formerly **Palazzo della Robbia** (number 15), was originally the home of the renowned Della Robbia family of artists. It was restructured in 1639 by G. B. Foggini. Further on, to the left, we come upon the tawny bulk of Palazzo Strozzi.

Left: Palazzo Strozzi - Façade; right: *Palazzo Spini-Ferroni*

STROZZI PALACE

Filippo Strozzi, a Florentine merchant of long-standing wealth (he had the merit of introducing into Tuscany not only the cultivation of artichokes, but also a good variety of fig), commissioned Benedetto da Maiano to build the palace in 1489; Benedetto was succeeded by Cronaca who directed the work until 1504. Later the construction was interrupted and resumed several times; the Strozzi family fell into disfavour in 1538, the palace was confiscated by Cosimo I dei Medici and given back thirty years later. Now it houses the Gabinetto Vieusseux and other cultural organisations; exhibitions are held here, as well as the **Biennial Antiques Exhibition Fair**. The massive building (by many considered the finest Renaissance building) has a stone plinth all round it at the base, projecting like a bench; the exterior recalls that of Palazzo Medici-Riccardi, with pronounced rustication; at the top is a magnificent cornice by Cronaca; the two upper storeys have fine mullioned, twin-arched windows; there is a majestic porticoed courtyard inside, also by Cronaca.

Piazza S. Trinita - Surrounded by noble mansions, the piazza is at the beginning of Via Tornabuoni, with the **Column of Justice** in the centre. This came from the Baths of Caracalla in Rome and supports the *Statue of Justice* by Francesco del Tadda (1581). The fine large battlemented palace that extends as far as Lungarno Acciaioli is the thirteenth-century **Palazzo Spini-Ferroni** (restored in the 19th cent.); at No. 1 of the piazza is **Palazzo Bartolini-Salimbeni**, Baccio d'Agnolo's masterpiece, with its unusual stone-cross partitioned windows (1520-23). The western side of the square is occupied by the church of Santa Trinita.

Church of Santa Trinita

CHURCH OF SANTA TRINITA

The church was built in the 11th cent. by the Vallombrosa monks. It was reconstructued in 1200 by Niccolò Pisano and was enlarged successively. The Mannerist façade is by Buontalenti (1593-94), whereas the *statue of St. Alexis* to the left and the bas relief with the *Holy Trinity* on the central portal are by Giovanni Caccini . The Gothic interior contains important art works of the 14th and 15th cents. Upon the inner façade you can see the remains of the original Romanesque church structure. Right aisle: on the altar of the third chapel, *Virgin and Child with Saints* by Neri di Bicci. The fourth chapel was painted by Lorenzo Monaco with *Scenes from the Life of Mary* and *Prophets* on the ceiling. On the altar is a panel painting of the *Annunciation*. Beyond the Sacristy is the **Sassetti Chapel** with its famous frescoed cycle by Domenico Ghirlandaio (1483-1486). High up on the wall outside the chapel, there is a *statue of David* painted upon a tall column. On the right, the *Tiburtine Sibyl Announcing the Birth of Christ to Augustus*. Four *Sibyls* are painted on the vault inside the chapel and *Episodes from the Life of St. Francis* on the walls. Starting from the upper left: 1) *St. Francis Giving up his Earthly Possessions*, 2) *Confirmation of the Franciscan Rule*, and 3) *Trial by Fire before the Sultan*. The lower register starting from the left shows: 4) *St. Francis Receiving the Stigmata*, to the right, 5) the *Death of St. Francis*; on the wall behind the altar: 6) *St. Francis, Invoked after his Death, Resuscitates a Youthful Member of the Spini Family*. Below are *portraits of Francesco Sassetti and his Wife*, Nera Corsi, who commissioned the work. Ghirlandaio's *Adoration of the Shepherds* (1495) is on the altar. The *tombs of Francesco and Nera Sassetti* attri-

81

Adoration of the Shepherds, by *Domenico Ghirlandaio*

buted to Giuliano da Sangallo (1491) flank the altar. In the adjoining chapel to the right of the presbytery is a huge *Crucifix*. It is known as the "Crucifix of St. Giovanni Gualberto". On the altar of the main chapel is an altarpiece with the *Holy Trinity and Saints* by Mariotto di Nardo (1416). In the left transept, in the second chapel to the left of the main one, is the exquisite carved marble *tomb of Benozzo Federighi, Bishop of Fiesole*, by Luca della Robbia (1456). Fifth chapel on the left aisle: wooden statue of the *Magdalen* by Desiderio da Settignano (1464), terminated by Benedetto da Maiano (1468). Next chapel: fifteenth-century Sienese school altarpiece with the *Coronation of the Virgin*. The third chapel contains a panel painting by Neri di Bicci of the *Annunciation,* set on the altar. The walls are frescoed with the *Disputation of St. Catherine,* by followers of Giotto.

Once outside the church, one turns right towards the **Bridge of Santa Trinita**. Built in 1252 and rebuilt several times, it now has the form given it by Bartolomeo Ammannati in 1567-70. At the ends are four statues of the *Seasons,* 1608. The most famous of these is the one representing *Spring*, by Pietro Francavilla (at the corner with Lungarno Acciaioli).

Bridge of Santa Trinita; below: *Palazzo Davanzati*

PALAZZO DAVANZATI

This stands in Via Porta Rossa, a narrow, picturesque street connecting Piazza Santa Trinita with Via Calzaioli, at the level of Piazza Davanzati. The palace, one of the finest and best preserved of the 14th cent., was built for the Davizzi family and passed in 1578 to the rich, powerful Davanzati family, who added various parts to it, including the loggia at the end. It now houses the interesting **Museo dell'Antica Casa Fiorentina** (Museum of the Ancient Florentine Home). There is a picturesque, porticoed courtyard, with a fine staircase leading up to the gallery round each storey. On the first floor is a hall with a fine cupboard for arms, a large table with an exquisite collection of caskets and some small fifteenth- and sixteenth-century terracotta busts of the Florentine school, and other furniture. The delightful **Parrot Room**, with walls painted with mock tapestry, with a fine fourteenth-century fireplace; a small drawing room, with furniture and paintings of the 16th cent.; the beautiful **Peacock Room**, with decorated walls, a fine tabernacle (15th cent.) and a carved sixteenth-century bedstead, which has a splendid and extremely rare white silk cover, embroidered with the *Story of Tristran* (14th-cent. Sicilian work). On the second floor, there is a hall like the first, with sixteenth-century furniture, a room of early sixteenth-century Florentine paintings, a study with fourteenth- and fifteenth-century paintings and two painted chests, the magnificent **Nuptial Chamber**, with fourteenth-century frescoes, two

83

tabernacles and a chest full of contemporary linen. Lastly, on the third floor, the **kitchen** containing various utensils, crockery, a small loom and a curious chandelier with oil lamps. Many of the rooms have fine wooden ceilings, some of which are beautifully decorated, and dressers containing fourteenth- to seventeenth-century pottery. There are also some "places of ease" - little rooms with old latrines. Some of the rooms in the basement of the palace are used for temporary craftswork and antique exhibitions.

Behind Palazzo Davanzati, off the parallel street known as Borgo Santissimi Apostoli we find Piazza del Limbo, so called because it was probably used as the burial-ground for unchristened babies (whose souls, according to the Church's doctrine, ended up in Limbo). In this piazza is the **Church of the Holy Apostles,** erected in the 11th cent. and rebuilt in the 16th. It still has its fine stone Romanesque façade with a Latin inscription (apocryphal) attributing the foundation of the church to Charlemagne. The interior has a nave and two side aisles, and a fine trussed ceiling; in the third chapel on the right is an *Immaculate Conception* by Vasari, with a fine fourteenth-century *polyptych* on the high altar; in the left aisle a large glazed terracotta *tabernacle* by Giovanni della Robbia and the *tomb of Oddo Altoviti*, by Benedetto da Rovezzano.

From Piazza Santa Trinita, one takes Via del Parione and after crossing Piazza Goldoni, one comes to Borgognissanti, leading into Piazza Ognissanti, where the **Church of Ognissanti** (All Saints), with its pleasant Baroque façade by Matteo Nigetti (1637) stands, overlooking the Arno. The church was restructured in the 17th cent. The belltower is 14th cent., however. Inside is the *Madonna of Mercy* frescoed by Ghirlandaio, commissioned by the Vespucci family (the future great navigator Amerigo, who lent his name to America, also appears in it), as well as the detached frescoes of *St. Jerome in his Study* by Ghirlandaio and *St. Augustine in his Study* by Botticelli (both 1480). The famous *Last Supper* by Ghirlandaio is in the **refectory**, left of the church.

Top: **Palazzo Davanzati**:
detail of the Nuptial Chamber;
above: *Church of Ognissanti*

Back once more in Piazza Goldoni, one turns left into Via dei Fossi, that leads up to spacious **Piazza Santa Maria Novella**, emerging into it at the corner of the **Loggia of St. Paul** (*c*.1490), decorated with della Robbia terracotta. On the other side of the square we can admire the façade of the great Dominican church of Santa Maria Novella.

Church of Santa Maria Novella

SANTA MARIA NOVELLA

The building was begun in 1221, designed by the architect friars Fra Sisto and Fra Ristoro. The lower part of the façade, first erected in 1300, was completed in the typical Florentine Romanesque-Gothic style before the middle of the 14th cent. After the middle of the 15th cent., Leon Battista Alberti, the great theorist of architecture, finished off the inlaid marble façade by adding the central doorway and the upper part, of extraordinary elegance, with a rose window, tympanum and side scrolls. The Cistercian Gothic **interior**, in the "softened" form that this style took in Italy, is in the shape of a Latin cross, with nave and side aisles and composite columns. An incredible number of art works decorate the walls and chapels. In the second bay of the right aisle is the *tomb of the Beata Villana*, by Bernardo Rossellino (1451). The right transept leads to the **Rucellai Chapel**; on the altar is a *Madonna* by Nino Pisano, in the floor the *tombstone of Leonardo Dati*, by Ghiberti (1425). The **Chapel of Filippo Strozzi** to the right of the high altar is covered with frescoes by Filippino Lippi (*c.*1500) with *Stories of SS. Philip and John the Evangelist*. The **Chancel** was frescoed by Domenico Ghirlandaio (*c.*1495, young Michelangelo was probably one of his assistants) with beautiful *Scenes of the Life of the Virgin*. The **Gondi Chapel** (left of the chancel) has the celebrated *Crucifix* by Brunelleschi, the only extant wooden sculpture of his. In the **Strozzi Chapel** (left transept) are frescoes by Nardo di Cione (*c.*1367; a remark-

Left: **Santa Maria Novella:** *interior;* right: *Holy Trinity,* by *Masaccio;*
below: **stained rose window with Crowning of the Virgin,** after a cartoon
by *Andrea di Bonaiuto*

able representation of *Hell*). In the **Sacristy** nearby is a *Crucifix*, a youthful work by Giotto. Lastly, at the third bay of the left aisle, the marvellous *Holy Trinity* by Masaccio (*c.* 1427) and the *pulpit* designed by Filippo Brunelleschi. Outside, to the right, is the interesting group of cloisters. The fourteenth-century **Green Cloister** has frescoes in the lunettes by fifteenth-century painters including Paolo Uccello, who painted the Scenes from Genesis (a very fine *Flood, c.* 1430). The **Spanish Chapel** is off the cloister, frescoed in the 14th cent. by Andrea di Bonaiuto, and used in the 16th cent. by Eleonora of Toledo's Spanish courtiers. Close by, in the **Chiostrino dei Morti,** a fourteenth century window with the *Crowning of the Virgin* closes the façade oculus.

Scenes of the Life of the Virgin (details), frescoes by *Ghirlandaio*;
below: *The Church Militant* (detail), fresco by *Andrea di Bonaiuto*

FIFTH ITINERARY

PIAZZA DEL DUOMO - CHURCH AND MUSEUM OF SAN MARCO ACADEMY GALLERY SANTISSIMA ANNUNZIATA - SPEDALE DEGLI INNOCENTI ARCHEOLOGICAL MUSEUM

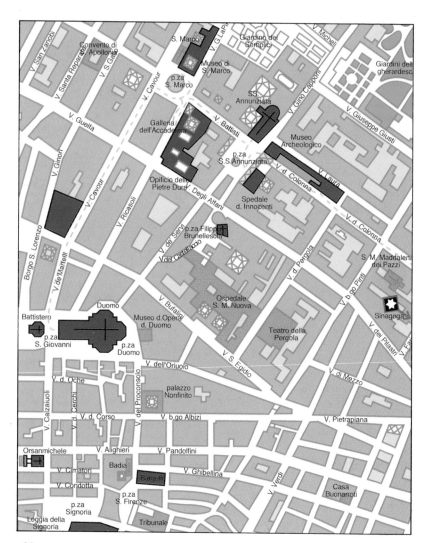

Via Cavour, one of the busiest thoroughfares in town, is flanked by severe seventeenth- and eighteenth-century mansions that give it a very stately appearance. It links Piazza del Duomo with Piazza della Libertà, traversing the left side of **Piazza San Marco**, which appears prevalently recently built. The only medieval note is the fourteenth-century loggia of the Accademia, once part of the former Hospital of St. Matthew, and now the entrance portico of the **Academy of Fine Arts**. On the corner with Via degli Arazzieri is the **Palazzina della Livia** (1775), built by Grand Duke Pietro Leopoldo for a circus dancer, Livia Malfatti. In the centre of the piazza are shrubs and trees and a *monument to General Manfredo Fanti*, by Pio Fedi (1873). One side of the piazza is occupied by the **Church** and **Monastery of San Marco**.

There had been a monastery of Silvestrini monks here since 1299; in the first half of the 15th cent., Cosimo the Elder assigned both the church and the monastery to the reformed Dominican monks of the Blessed Giovanni Dominici; this was partly at the behest of Pope Eugene IV, and partly in expiation of Cosimo's own misdeeds. He commissioned Michelozzo to carry out the work of restoration, and invested 40,000 florins in it. In the following centuries there were several alterations, particularly to the church, which has a neo-Renaissance façade of the 18th century. The interior was re-structured by Giambologna in 1588 and by Silvani in 1678; on the interior façade is a *Crucifix* by followers of Giotto. At the third altar on the right, the *Virgin in Prayer* is a ninth century mosaic. Of interest are the St Anthoninus and Sacrament Chapels.

Coat of arms of the Silk Guild;
below: **Church of San Marco**,
façade

Below: *Flight to Egypt* (detail),
by *Fra Angelico*

89

Annunciation, by *Fra Angelico*

MUSEUM OF SAN MARCO

The entrance to the monastery of San Marco is beside the church, one of the most important centres in Florence in the 15th cent. because of the protection granted to it by Cosimo the Elder and Lorenzo the Magnificent and also because of the unquestioned authority of its prior, St. Anthoninus. Savonarola, Fra Angelico and Fra Bartolomeo all lived there. Fra Angelico was one of the greatest artists of the 15th cent. He infused Masaccio's newly rediscovered rules of perspective with a spirit that was still Gothic, to express a mystical, contemplative religious experience. The **Cloister of St. Anthoninus**, by Michelozzo, has frescoed lunettes and some interesting rooms give onto it. The **Pilgrims' Hospice** contains an exceptional series of panel paintings by Fra Angelico: the *Linen Merchant's Tabernacle*, the *Altar-piece from the Convent of Bosco ai Frati*, the *Annalena Altar-piece*, the *Descent from the Cross*, the *Last Judgement*. The **Chapter-house** contains a magnificent *Crucifixion* by Fra Angelico. The artist also decorated the **Dormitory** on the first floor between 1439 and 1445; each cell, fascinating in its simplicity, is adorned with master pieces, like the *Annunciation, Noli me tangere*, the *Transfiguration* and the *Coronation of the Virgin*. In the **Prior's Apartment** is a *Portrait of Savonarola*, who lived here, by his disciple Fra Bartolomeo.

The Tribune, by *Emilio de' Fabris;* below: *the floor pattern*

GALLERY OF THE ACADEMY

This is one of the most famous galleries in Italy, visited by thousands of people, especially owing to the presence of the *David* and of other famous sculptures by Michelangelo. The Gallery (Via Ricasoli 60, near Piazza San Marco) was founded in 1784 by Grand Duke Peter Leopold of Hapsburg Lorraine as an Academy of Fine Arts, to unite all the schools of art drawing and sculpture already existing in the city. The gallery was thus created with the specific purpose of helping the pupils to know and to study the Old Masters.

Many of the pieces came, however, from a previous collection that belonged to the Academy of the Art of Drawing, an institution of great prestige, founded in 1562 by Cosimo I. This included all the greatest artists of the time, and was based on the fourteenth-century Company of Painters of St. Luke. The already

The *Hall of the Colossus* with *Rape of the Sabines,* by *Giambologna;* below: *David* (detail). Opposite: *David;* top right: *Palestrina Pietà;* bottom left and right: *Two of the Four Prisoners,* all by *Michelangelo*

considerable collection of paintings was increased as a result of the suppression of churches and monasteries (1786 and 1808); there were further acquisitions and in 1873 the *David* was brought here, followed in 1911 by the *Prisoners* and *St. Matthew,* while the *Pietà* only arrived in 1939, when it was bought by the State. The Gallery also exhibits a plaster model of the *Rape of the Sabines* by Giambologna as well as a notable collection of paintings from the 13th till the early 16th cent.; among the most important works are: a *Crucifix,* Sienese school, second half of the 13th cent. (attributed by some to the great Duccio di Buoninsegna); the *Tree of the Cross,* by Pacino di Buonaguida (early 14th cent.); a *polyptych* by Andrea Orcagna (mid 14th cent.) and works by his brothers, including a *triptych* by Nardo di Cione (1365) and a *Coronation of the Virgin* by Jacopo di Cione; twenty-four panels by Taddeo Gaddi (fourteen with *Scenes of the Life of Christ* and ten with *Scenes of the Life of St. Francis;* the very fine *Pietà* by Giovanni da Milano (1365); the *Adimari Chest;* a *Visitation* attributed to Domenico Ghirlandaio; the *Madonna of the Sea* and the youthful *Madonna and Child, Little St. John and Two Angels,* by Sandro Botticelli; *Trinity and Saints,* by Alesso Baldovinetti (1471).

Going back to Piazza San Marco, we turn right into Via Cesare Battisti, which leads into **Piazza Santissima Annunziata**. This elegant square is surrounded on three sides by porticoes. On the right, the **Spedale degli Innocenti**, at right angles to the **Church of the Santissima Annunziata**. The entrance to the **Archaeological Museum** is in Via Colonna (on the left), the road between the church and the Hospital, beneath the arch. Left, the **Palace of the Servants of Mary**, designed in 1525 by Antonio da Sangallo and Baccio d'Agnolo to resemble the Hospital of the Innocents. The building on the corner of Via dei Servi on the left is **Palazzo Grifoni**, by Ammannati (1563). In the centre is the *Statue of Grand Duke Ferdinando I,* begun by Giambologna and finished by Tacca (1608) who made the two fountains on either side (1629).

Church of the Santissima Annunziata

SANTISSIMA ANNUNZIATA

In 1250, seven young Florentines, later beatified as the Seven Holy Founders, set up the order of the Servants of Mary, and began to build a shrine dedicated to the Virgin. The church was rebuilt by Michelozzo in the 15th cent. and later by Antonio Manetti who, together with Leon Battista Alberti, was responsible for the design of the circular choir at the end of the aisleless nave. The porch on the piazza is late 16th century. Between this and the church is the **Cloister of Vows**, decorated with fine early sixteenth-century frescoes by Andrea del Sarto, and other Mannerist artists.

To the left of the entrance, just inside the church (restored and embellished in the Baroque period) is a small fifteenth-century temple, that contains a greatly-venerated fourteenth-century *Annunciation*, which is supposed to have been painted partly by an angel. Among the many works of art, mention should be made of two *lecterns* in the form of eagles (15th-century English work). In the elegant tribune, *Jesus and St. Julian* by Andrea del Castagno (*c*. 1455, first altar on the left) and the *Trinity* by the same (second altar on the left). Beside the church are the buildings of the Monastery which include the **Cloister of the Dead**, frescoed with *Stories of the Servants of Mary* by Florentine Mannerist artists.

Piazza Santissima Annunziata with the church and the Spedale degli Innocenti; below: *Della Robbia terracotta tile*

SPEDALE DEGLI INNOCENTI

In 1419 the Guild of Silk Merchants decided to purchase a piece of land and build a hospital for foundlings or "Innocents". Brunelleschi was commissioned to provide the plan, which determined the architecture of the whole piazza onto which the hospital faces, creating a portico whose proportions, in relation to the rest, required the uniformity of all the surrounding buildings. We can see here how the Renaissance conception of "planning" replaced the casual building that went on in the Middle Ages, when one building was put up beside another in a completely different style. The hospital was finished in 1457. The front consists of nine wide arches on columns that stand at the top of a flight of steps. Above these, a low upper storey which has windows with tympanums. Between the arches, glazed terracotta *putti* (babies) by Andrea della Robbia (*c.* 1487). Two pilaster strips close the portico at the sides.

Inside: the exquisitely simple cloisters by Brunelleschi and a collection of works mostly of the 15th cent. The collection includes: an *Annunciation* by Giovanni del Biondo; *Madonna and Child with Saints* by Piero di Cosimo; *Adoration of the Magi* by Ghirlandaio (1488); a *Madonna and Child with Angels* by the school of Perugino; the *Madonna of the Innocents*, attributed to Pontormo.

Chimaera (4th cent. B.C.); below: *François Vase*

ARCHAEOLOGICAL MUSEUM

Cosimo the Elder was a keen collector of coins, goldsmiths' work and antique sculpture, a passion shared by the later Medici. The Hapsburg-Lorraine family started the Egyptian antiquities section and encouraged independent excavation. In 1828 Leopold II subsidised an archaeological expedition in Egypt and Nubia, led by the Frenchman Champollion and the Italian Rossellini. In 1880 the collection was housed in its present seat, Palazzo della Crocetta in Via della Colonna, built by Giulio Parigi in 1820. The museum is divided into three sections: the Etrurian Topographical Museum, the Etrusco-Graeco-Roman Antiquities, and the Egyptian Museum. On the ground floor, the rooms are arranged didactically: the famous *François Vase* and the *Mater Matuta* are kept here. The pleasant garden contains reconstructions (partly with authentic materials) of funeral monuments and Etruscan tombs.

The Egyptian Museum is on the first floor. Among the most interesting exhibits: the two statuettes of handmaidens intent on domestic

Left: Mater Matuta,(Etruscan sculpture, 5th cent. B.C.); right: *limestone statue,* (Egyptian art, 2400 B.C.); below: *Egyptian stele*

work; the *statue of Thutmosis III* (1490-1436 BC); the *"Fayyum" Portrait of a Woman* (2nd cent. AD); painted slabs, stelae, sarcophagi, mummies and a war chariot. Also on the first floor, among the Antiquities, Attic kouroi of the 6th cent. BC; Etruscan funeral urns; a *Statue of the Orator* (c. 100 BC); Etruscan sarcophagi; the *Chimera of Arezzo*; the *Little Idol*; Attic vases and Etruscan buccheri. Pre-Roman and Italic finds, along with those from Magna Grecia, are on the upper floors.

Turning right out of the Museum, one encounters **Benvenuto Cellini's House**. Here the great goldsmith-sculptor modelled and cast the famous *Perseus*, now sheltered in the Uffizi.

- The street leads into a pleasantly landscaped square, **Piazza d'Azeglio**. Turning right into Via Farini we come to the **Synagogue** of Florence at number 6. Funded by David Levi's donation to the Jewish University, it was designed by a team of architects (Mariano Falcini, Marco Treves, and Vincenzo Micheli) and built between 1872 and 1874. Oriental in style, it has a lovely copper-covered dome and well-designed windows.

97

SIXTH ITINERARY

....

PIAZZA DEL DUOMO -BARGELLO MUSEUM
BADIA FIORENTINA -BUONARROTI HOUSE
CHURCH AND MUSEUM OF SANTA CROCE

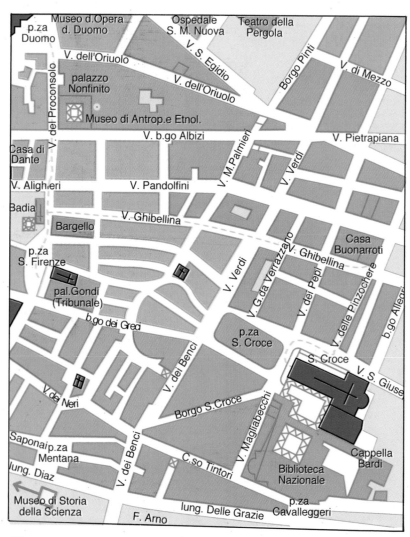

Via del Proconsolo, which from Piazza del Duomo leads to Piazza San Firenze, contains a number of interesting buildings. As well as the Bargello and the Badia, N° 10 is the **Pazzi Palace**, built between 1462 and 1472 for this family, who soon afterwards plotted the famous conspiracy against the Medici. At N° 12 is the **Palazzo Nonfinito,** started by Buontalenti for the Strozzi family in 1592. This now houses the **Museum of Anthropology and Ethnology,** founded by Paolo Mantegazza in 1869, the first of its kind in Italy. The most interesting things are: the wooden statue of a native of Patagonia, ordered by the Grand Duke of Tuscany at the end of the 18th cent., (it is over eight feet high, modelled according to the fanciful description given at the time by a sea-captain; African handicrafts; wooden sculptures of that mysterious people, the Kafirs (from the Karakorum); Amazonian ornaments, an Eskimo kayak; masks from Oceania; arms from Malay; mummies of the Incas and religious objects from Tibet.

A side street off the Proconsolo (Via Dante Alighieri) leads to the **House of Dante**, a medieval building restored in the 19th cent. which is part of a group of houses that belonged to the Alighieri family. The museum has ample documentation on fourteenth-century Florence, including portraits of the poet and some rare editions of the *Divine Comedy.*

Not far off (quite near Piazza della Signoria), is the fairly narrow **Piazza San Firenze**, dominated by two large buildings of differing styles and periods: **Palazzo Gondi,** by Giuliano da Sangallo (1490-1501), and, opposite, that very fine example of Florentine Baroque, the great complex of the ex-Convent of San Firenze (17th and 18th centuries) - the seat of the Tribunal of Justice.

Above: *Bakers' Guild coat of arms;* below: *House of Dante;* bottom: *Palazzo del Bargello in Piazza San Firenze*

Left: *the Bargello "Prison" in a nineteenth-century print;*
right: *Verrocchio's* **David***; below: Donatello's* **David**

MUSEO NAZIONALE (BARGELLO)

This is the most important Italian museum of sculpture and minor arts. It is housed in the severe, square Palazzo del Bargello, a thirteenth-century building of great historical importance, that was begun in 1255 and was first used as the seat of the Captain of the People. After 1574 it was the seat of the Captain of Justice, or "Bargello" (that is the chief of police) and the palace became notorious for the executions held there. The Museum was founded in 1865. A description of the principal works must begin with the splendid **courtyard**, under the arches of which there is a large and very fine cannon of the early 17th cent. and, among the sculptures, the delightful *Fisherboy* by Vincenzo Gemito (1877). One of the rooms on the ground floor contains such masterpieces by Michelangelo as the *bust of Brutus* (1539), who was seen at that time as a heroic liberator from tyranny, the so-called *Pitti Tondo* (*c.* 1504), rendered with the characteristic and expressive "unfinished" style; the *David-Apollo* (*c.*1531), delicate and harmonious; and the youthful *Drunken Bacchus* (1496-97). In the same room we have another *Bacchus* by Sansovino (1520) and the *Bronze Bust of Cosimo I*, exquisitely modelled by Benvenuto Cellini (1545-47), as well as Giambologna's famous *Mer-*

cury. On the first floor, on the fine **balcony**, are more bronzes by Giambologna. In the **Donatello Hall**, besides masterpieces by the great fifteenth-century sculptor, are numerous terracotta works by Luca della Robbia and the panels with the *Sacrifice of Isaac* by Brunelleschi and Ghiberti. The other rooms display splendid majolica pottery from Faenza and other provenances, enamels, goldsmiths' work, liturgical objects and valuable ivories of various periods. On the second floor: a room with terracotta items by Giovanni della Robbia and one with those by his father Andrea; a room devoted to Verrocchio that also contains lovely works by Laurana, Mino da Fiesole, Benedetto Maiano, Rossellino and Pollaiolo; lastly, two rooms with small bronzes (and a huge, stupendous 15th century fireplace) and arms.

Bust of Cosimo I de' Medici, by *B. Cellini*; below: *section of the courtyard*

BADIA FIORENTINA

Opposite the Bargello, in Via del Proconsolo, is the entrance to the church of the Badia. Founded in the tenth cent., it was rebuilt in 1285 by Arnolfo di Cambio, and again in 1627 by Matteo Segaloni. The elegant hexagonal **belltower** is 14th cent. The fine fifteenth/sixteenth-century doorway leads into a porticoed courtyard, where the entrance to the church is. To the left of the entrance is the remarkable, finely-detailed masterpiece by Filippino Lippi, the *Madonna Appears to St. Bernard* (*c.*1485). In the right transept is the *monument to Bernardo Giugni*, by Mino da Fiesole (*c.*1470); in the opposite transept, by the same sculptor, is the *monument to Count Ugo* (1469-81) whose mother founded the Badia. To the right of the presbytery is the entrance to the sacristy, from which one goes out into the **Cloister "of the Orange Trees"** built in 1432-38 by Bernardo Rossellino. This quiet, elegant cloister has two orders of arches and the lunettes in the upper gallery are frescoed with lively *Scenes from the Life of St. Benedict*, a fifteenth-century work attributed to the Portuguese painter, Giovanni di Consalvo.

Via Ghibellina starts at the corner, opposite the church of the Badia Fiorentina. At No. 70 we find the Buonarroti House.

BUONARROTI HOUSE

This attractive fifteenth-century building is not Michelangelo's real birthplace. He was actually born to a noble family of Florentine origin on 6 March 1475 at Caprese in the Casentino district, where his father had been sent to act as mayor. The house in Florence was bought by Michelangelo (though he never lived there) for his nephew Leonardo. Subsequently, the artist's great nephew (and a distinguished man of letters), Michelangelo Buonarroti the Younger, had some rooms redecorated, commissioned some of the best-known Florentine painters of his time, including Giovanni da San Giovanni, Empoli, Matteo Rosselli, Francesco Furini and Artemisia Gentileschi, to paint scenes of the apotheosis of Michelangelo. An array of rooms contain works by Michelangelo, including his first sculptures (one of the San Lorenzo façade) and also drawings, models and bozzetti (the most important being a *model of Rijeka*). Among works by other artists (copies of Michelangelo's oeuvres and portraits of members of the Buonarroti family), of interest is a predella with *Stories of St. Nicholas of Bari*, by Giovanni di Francesco (15th cent.), a *Narcissus* attributed to Paolo Uccello, and a *Love Scene*, an early work by Titian.

Michelangelo presenting Pope Pio IV with the model of St Peter's,
by *Passignano;* right: *Allegory of Inclination,* by *A. Gentileschi;*
below: *Madonna of the Steps,* by *Michelangelo.*
Opposite: **Buonarroti Family Coat of Arms**

Almost opposite Casa Buonarroti, Via delle Pinzochere leads into **Piazza Santa Croce**. Ever since the Middle Ages this piazza had been the scene of festivities, tournaments, meetings, games - famous is the tournament between Lorenzo and Giuliano dei Medici. St. Bernardino da Siena also preached here, the Carnival took place here and the traditional football in costume is indeed still played here. In 1865 Enrico Pazzi placed the *monument to Dante* (later transferred to the front of the church) in the middle of the square. On the south side of the piazza is **Palazzo dell'Antella**, the façade of which, on corbels, was frescoed in the space of three weeks by twelve painters directed by Giovanni da San Giovanni (17th cent.). A *bust of Cosimo II* is above the door. Between two windows on the ground floor is a sixteenth-century marble disc indicating the centre of the piazza for the football game. The classical façade of the **Palazzo Cocchi-Serristori** opposite the church is attributed to Baccio d'Agnolo (16th cent.)

103

Santa Croce Church

SANTA CROCE

This church originated as a small oratory, built by a community of monks in 1228. In 1294 Arnolfo di Cambio began the construction of the present basilica, in the monumental, soberly decorated style that characterises Franciscan churches. The church was consecrated in 1443 in the presence of Pope Eugene IV. In 1566 Giorgio Vasari, commissioned by Cosimo I, designed the altars in the side aisles; this involved destroying the old choir and numerous frescoes. The **façade** of the church was only added in the mid 19th cent. and was designed by Nicolò Matas in neo-Gothic style (like the belltower built by Gaetano Baccani in 1847). The extraordinary importance of this church, with its numerous art works, is enhanced by the many tombs of illustrious men (the "Urns of the Strong" celebrated by Ugo Foscolo in the *Sepolcri.*) The **interior** has a nave and two side aisles, with pointed arches supported by octagonal stone pillars. The floor is studded with no fewer than 276 tombstones, the oldest being 14th cent. In the central nave, at the third pillar on the right, is the fine marble *pulpit* by Benedetto da Maiano (1472-76); the square panels relate *Episodes from the Life of St. Francis.* In the right aisle, at the first pillar, the *Madonna 'del Latte'* by Rossellino (1478); opposite, the *Funeral Monument to Michelangelo* by Vasari and helpers (1570); the crouching female figures represent the *Muses of Painting, Sculpture* and *Architecture.* Next come

Interior; below: ***Wooden Crucifix***, *by Donatello*

the *Cenotaph of Dante Alighieri* (buried at Ravenna) by Stefano Ricci (1829); the *tomb of Vittorio Alfieri*, by Canova in 1810; the *tomb of Niccolò Machiavelli*, by Spinazzi (1787); the splendid *Annunciation* by Donatello (*c.* 1435); the *monument to Leonardo Bruni*, by Rossellino (*c.* 1444); the *tomb of Gioacchino Rossini* and that of *Ugo Foscolo*. In the right transept, on the right, is the **Castellani Chapel**, frescoed about 1385 by Agnolo Gaddi with *Stories of St. Nicholas of Bari, John the Baptist* and *Anthony Abbot*. At the end of the transept is the entrance to the **Baroncelli Chapel,** frescoed with *Stories of the Virgin* by Taddeo Gaddi (1332-38); on the altar a polyptych with the *Coronation of the Virgin*, from the workshop of Giotto. At the corner of the transept is the entrance to the fine fourteenth-century **Sacristy;** on the right wall, three episodes from the *Passion* by Taddeo Gaddi and others; in the end wall is the entrance to the **Rinuccini Chapel,** with frescoes by Giovanni da Milano. Returning to the church, one should visit the chapels at the east end; the **Peruzzi Chapel** (fourth from the right) has splendid frescoes by Giotto with *Stories of the Baptist* and *St. John the Evangelist.* The **Bardi Chapel** (the fifth) has *Stories of St. Francis*, also by Giotto; this cycle is to be placed among the painter's

105

Left: *Monument to Michelangelo Buonarroti*, by *Vasari*; right: *Cenotaph of Dante*, by *Stefano Ricci*; below: *Sacristy*, with frescoes by *Taddeo Gaddi*, *Spinello Aretino and Niccolò Gerini*

masterpieces (*c.*1325). The **Chancel** has frescoes by Agnolo Gaddi and a *polyptych* by Niccolo Gerini (late 14th cent.). Of the left transept chapels, the **Bardi di Vernio Chapel** has fine *Stories of St. Sylvester*, by Maso di Banco (*c.*1340). The Bardi Chapel at the head of the transept has a *Crucifix* by Donatello (*c.*1425).

Funeral of St. Francis, by *Giotto;* below left: *Annunciation,* by *Donatello;*
below right: *Episodes from the Life of St. Francis,* by *an anonymous Florentine*

On the left, the **Salviati Chapel** with the nineteenth-century *tomb of Sofia Zamoyski* by Lorenzo Bartolini. The series of funeral monuments continues in the left aisle; note the *tomb of Carlo Marsuppini*, by Deside-rio Settignano (*c*.1453) and that of *Galileo Galilei* by Giulio Foggini (18th cent.).

Pazzi Chapel

SANTA CROCE MUSEUM

This is housed in part of the Monastery of Santa Croce. The entrance lies to the right of the church. The first, and most important room is the old fourteenth-century **Refectory**, the end wall of which is covered by an enormous fresco by Taddeo Gaddi representing the *Tree of Life*, the *Last Supper* and other scenes. On the right wall is Cimabue's magnificent *Crucifix*, painted on wood and badly damaged in the 1966 flood, and three fragments of the *Triumph of Death* frescoed by Orcagna on the walls of Santa Croce (found under Vasari's altars, they were then detached). On the left is the *St. Ludovic* in gilded bronze by Donatello (1423). The other rooms contain remains of fourteenth and fifteenth-century glass windows, Della Robbia terracotta artefacts, works by Andrea del Castagno, Agnolo Bronzino, Giorgio Vasari and others. The harmonious façade of the **Pazzi Chapel** acts as back-drop to the first cloister. Filippo Brunelleschi designed the building in *c*. 1430; he worked on it at intervals until 1444, when other architects took over.

Crucifix, on wood by *Cimabue*

A pronaos preceding the entrance has six Corinthian columns and a wide central arch between elegant inset panels in grey sandstone; the frieze with heads of *cherubs* is by Desiderio da Settignano. The chapel dome has a conical covering (1461) and under the portico the smaller dome was decorated with glazed terracotta by Luca della Robbia, who also executed the tondo of *St. Andrew* above the door, the panels of which are splendidly carved by Giuliano da Maiano (1472). The rectangular interior has the geometric clarity and measured rhythm of the best Brunelleschi creation: white walls, grooved pilaster strips in grey stone, wide arches and the brightly-coloured tondi by Luca della Robbia, with figures of *Apostles* and *Evangelists*.

Leaving Santa Croce, we turn left into Via Magliabechi. Along the left side of the street is the west wing of the **National** (State) **Library** (entrance at Piazza Cavalleggeri l). This is Italy's most important library, known the world over. At the end of Corso Tintori, the street intersecting Via Magliabechi, we turn left into Via de' Benci. The first building on the left is **Palazzo degli Alberti e dei Corsi**, attributed to Giuliano da Sangallo, now seat of the Horne Foundation.

SEVENTH ITINERARY

VII

• •

VIALE DEI COLLI - PIAZZALE MICHELANGELO
SAN MINIATO AL MONTE - FORTE BELVEDERE
FIESOLE

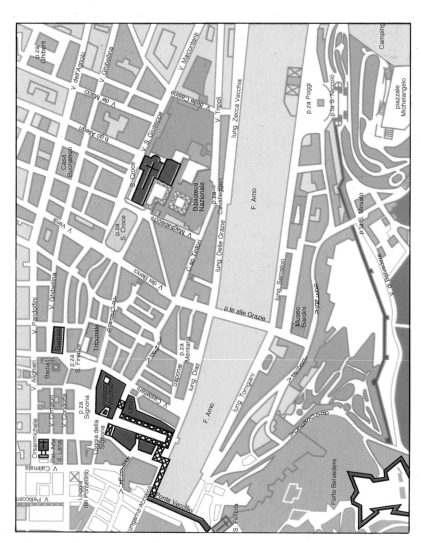

PIAZZALE MICHELANGELO

O n the other side of the Arno, one climbs up the Viale dei Colli that winds its way for almost six kilometres along the hills lying south of the town (one can also walk up the "Rampe" that start at Porta San Niccolò), until one reaches the wide viewpoint or terrace that surveys the whole town and the surrounding hillsides: Piazzale Michelangelo. This splendid esplanade was planned by Giuseppe Poggi in the 1860s, as a spectacular climax to his great rearrangement of Florence, at that time capital of Italy. In the centre of the square is the *Monument to Michelangelo*, cast in 1875, with copies in bronze of some of his marble statues. Going on up the hill behind is the little **church of San Salvatore al Monte**, begun in 1495 by Cronaca.

Monument to Michelangelo;
below: *Forte Belvedere*

Church of San Miniato al Monte

SAN MINIATO AL MONTE

O ne of the oldest and most beautiful churches in Florence. A wide marble staircase leads up to it from nearby Piazzale Michelangelo. An ancient oratory, dedicated to St. Minias, reputedly martyred on that hill in the 4th cent., was incorporated into the Romanesque church between the 11th and 13th cent. The **façade** is faced with green and white marble. The fine mosaic in the centre (13th cent., much restored) represents *Christ between the Virgin and St. Minias*; at the top

Church of San Miniato al Monte: *Interior*

of the tympanum, an *Eagle*, symbol of the Guild of Woolmerchants who subsidised the upkeep of the church. The **interior** has a nave and two side aisles, with a crypt and a raised presbytery above it. The floor of the nave is inlaid with splendid marble panels. In the centre, between the two flights of steps leading up to the presbytery, is the **Crucifix Chapel** by Michelozzo (1448), commissioned by Piero the Gouty, with a delightful multicoloured timbered and majolica vault by Luca della Robbia and altar panels by Agnolo Gaddi. From the left aisle one enters the **Chapel of the Cardinal of Portugal**, one of the most elegant creations of the Florentine Renaissance, by Antonio Manetti (1461-66), a pupil of Brunelleschi; this contains the *Tomb of Jacopo Di Lusitania*, archbishop of Lisbon, by Rossellino; fine della Robbia terracottas on the vault, a splendid *Annunciation* by Baldovinetti (on the left) and two *Angels* frescoed by Antonio and Piero del Pollaiolo (on the wall opposite the entrance, above the copy of the *Saints Eustace, James* and *Vincent* by the Pollaiolo brothers, original at the Uffizi). On the vault of the crypt, above the altar, are frescoes of *Saints and Prophets* by Taddeo Gaddi. The presbytery of the church is surrounded with a fine thirteenth-century marble transenna and a splendid *pulpit*; on the right altar is a painting on wood by Jacopo del Casentino with *St. Minias and Eight Scenes from his Life*. The mosaic in the apse represents *Christ Enthroned between the Virgin, St. Minias and the Symbols of the Evangelists* (1279, but restored in 1491 by Baldovinetti). From the Presbytery one turns right into the **Sacristy**, frescoed after 1387 by Spinello Aretino, with *Stories of St. Benedict*. To the right of the church is the **Bishops' Palace** (13th to 14th cent.). Round the church are the walls of the Fortress constructed by Michelangelo in 1529 to defend Florence during the siege by the Spanish army of Charles V.

Piazza Mino

Via San Leonardo - One of the most charming country roads of Florence, leading off the Viale dei Colli. Grey-green olive trees peep over the old stone walls and lovely villas into the narrow lane. Halfway down, on the right, is a charming Romanesque church, **San Leonardo in Arcetri**, inside which are fourteenth-century paintings of the Tuscan school and a Romanesque marble pulpit (13th cent.). Before ending at the **Porta San Giorgio** (1324), the road turns left into the grounds of **Forte Belvedere**, which was built between 1590 and 1595 by Giovanni de' Medici and Bernardo Buontalenti. Its ramparts command a superb view of the city below. International art shows and other cultural events are periodically held here.

FIESOLE

A charming little town about five miles north of Florence, it was founded by the Etruscans in the 7th cent. BC. Three centuries later it was colonised by the Romans. After the fall of the Empire it was an important bishopric, then in the 12th cent. it succumbed to its stronger neighbour, Florence. After losing all its political power, it eventually became a favourite summer resort for rich Florentines (the Medicis had a villa here) and, in the 18th cent., foreign visitors, especially the English also came here. The centre of the little town is the wide **Piazza Mino**, where the principal public buildings are. The **Cathedral** was built in 1028 and later enlarged. In the **Salutati Chapel** are frescoes by Cosimo Rosselli and the tomb of *Bishop Leonardo Salutati*, by Mino da Fiesole, 15th cent.

Roman Theatre

On the High Altar is a *triptych* by Bicci di Lorenzo (*c.* 1440). In the crypt, which is Romanesque, are fifteenth-century frescoes by Benedetto di Nanni, a *baptismal font* by Francesco del Tadda (16th cent.) and the *Wooden Bishop's Chair of St. Andrea Corsini* (14th cent.). The **Bandini Museum** nearby has interesting Della Robbia terracottas and works by Agnolo and Taddeo Gaddi, Lorenzo Monaco and Jacopo del Sellaio. Also in Piazza Mino is the **Praetorian Palace** (15th cent.) with façade and loggia covered with coats of arms. Near the piazza is the **Roman Theatre** (1st cent. BC) which seats an audience of 3000 and is still in use for summer concerts and other events. In the vicinity of the theatre are the remains of a temple (first Etruscan and later Roman) and some Roman baths. The **Archaeological Museum** beside the area of excavation contains relics of Etruscan and Roman Fiesole; urns from Chiusi and Volterra; storied stelae, typical of the zone; Greek vases, objects in bucchero, small bronzes and other sculptures. Returning to the piazza, one goes up a very steep little road to **Sant'Alessandro**, an ancient church standing on the site of an Etruscan temple. A little beyond it are the church and **Monastery of San Francesco**; this church was built between the 14th and 15th cent., and has a simple façade with a rose window and porched entrance. The interior is Gothic with a single nave; the High Altar has a beautiful *Annunciation* by Raffaellino del Garbo (early 16th cent.); at the second altar on the left, *Madonna and Saints* by the school of Perugino; next to it, an *Immaculate Conception* by Cosimo Rosselli. The fine inlaid *choir* is early 16th cent. Right of the church is the small **Cloister of St. Bernardino** (13th to 14th cent.). Half way between Fiesole and Florence is the **Church of San Domenico** built in the 15th cent. but restored in the 17th; it contains a *Madonna and Child with Angels and Saints* (*c.* 1430) by Fra Angelico, who was prior of the nearby monastery.

*U*SEFUL INFORMATION

EMERGENCY TELEPHONE NUMBERS
TOURIST INFORMATION
CONSULATES
OVERNIGHT CHEMISTS
HOSPITALS
TRAVEL AGENTS
HOSTELS AND CAMP SITES
MUSEUMS AND ART GALLERIES
SECOND WORLD WAR CEMETERIES
NON-CATHOLIC CHURCHES
WORSHIP IN ENGLISH
BANKS
LIBRARIES
MARKETS
POST OFFICE
HOTELS
RESTAURANTS
TRATTORIE
CHINESE RESTAURANTS
PIZZAS AND SANDWICHES
CAFÉS
FLORENCE BY NIGHT (DISCOS)
PIANO BARS AND NIGHT CLUBS
CINEMAS AND THEATRES
USEFUL HINTS

NOTIZIE UTILI

The end section of the guide has a compendium of practical information concerning museums, hotels, public and private transport and anything of usde to the visitor to Florence. Signs placed along main tourist routes indicate the more important sights and museums.

(EMERGENCY TELEPHONE NUMBERS

A C I.- Road assistance	☎	116
Ambulance Service	☎	212222
or	☎	215555
Car service	☎	24861
Carabinieri Emergency Calls	☎	112
Cardiological Emergency	☎	214444
Central Railway Station	☎	2351
Chemists open	☎	192
Customs	☎	214316
Fire Brigade	☎	115
Florence Vespucci Airport	☎	373498
Lost Property Office	☎	367943
Medical Emergency Service	☎	118
Municipal Police	☎	36911
Pisa Galilei Airport	☎	050/500707
Police Emergency Calls	☎	113
Police Headquarters	☎	49771
Post Office and Telecommunication Services	☎	160
Radio Taxi	4390 - 4798 - 424 2 - 4386	
Railway Information	☎	288785
Rail-Station Luggage Service	☎	212319
Road conditions	☎	4477
Road Police	☎	577777
Unclaimed Property Office	☎	2352190
Urban bus transport	☎	5650222

▲ LOST PROPERTY

Lost property is taken to the relevant municipal office in Via Circondaria 19 (367943), the Central Police Station (49771), the Carabinieri (112) and the Railway Police Offices (212296). Items left on taxis can be claimed from the Municipal Police or City Council Offices.

⑦ TOURIST INFORMATION

Tourist Information (APT)	☎	23320
City and Provincial Info	☎	290832
Hotel Information Syndicate	☎	282893
Tourist S.O.S. Florence	☎	22760382

🏛 CONSULATES

Austria - V. dei Servi, 9	☎	2382008
Belgium - V. dei Servi, 28	☎	282094
Bolivia - V.Torre del Gallo, 24	☎	220017
Brasil - V. Masaccio, 60	☎	222336
China - V. Fontana	☎	216689
Cile - V. L. Alamanni, 25	☎	214131
Costa Rica - V. Giambologna	☎	573603
Denmark - V. dei Servi, 13	☎	211007
Finland - V. Strozzi, 6	☎	293228
France - P.zza Ognissanti	☎	2302556
Germany - L.no Vespucci, 30	☎	294722
Great Britain - L.no Corsini, 2	☎	212594
Haiti - V. Cerretani, 2	☎	282683
Hungary - V. Belgio, 2	☎	6531817
Malta - V. dei Servi, 13	☎	217875
Mexico - V. Arte della Lana	☎	217831
Netherlands - V. Cavour, 81	☎	475249
Norway - V. G. Capponi, 26	☎	2479321
Panama - V. Respighi, 8	☎	351493
Perù - V. della Mattonaia, 17	☎	2343345
San Marino - V. Roma, 3	☎	210864
South Africa - P.zza Saltarelli	☎	281863
Spain - V. G. La Pira, 21	☎	217110
Sweden - V. della Scala, 4	☎	2396865
Switzerland - P.le Galileo, 5	☎	222434
Turkey - V. Nazionale, 7	☎	294893
U. S. of America - L.no Vespucci	☎	294921
Venezuela - V .Giambologna	☎	588082

✚ OVERNIGHT CHEMISTS

Bargioni
V. G. Orsini, 107r ☎ 6811616
Codecà
V. Ginori, 50r ☎ 210849
Comunale N°5
P.zza dell'Isolotto, 5 ☎ 710293
Comunale N°6
V.le Calatafimi, 6r ☎ 600945
Comunale N°8
V.le Guidoni, 89r ☎ 415546
Del Galluzzo
V. Senese, 206r ☎ 2049217
Della Nave
P.zza delle Cure, 2r ☎ 573717
Di Rifredi
P.zza Dalmazia, 24r ☎ 4360800
Morelli
V. G. Orsini, 27r ☎ 6812145
Mungai
V. Starnina, 41 r ☎ 7398595
Paglicci
V. della Scala, 61r ☎ 215612
Paoletti
V. di Brozzi, 282a ☎ 317248

✛ HOSPITALS

General Hospital of S. Maria Nuova
P.zza S. M. Nuova, 1 ☎ 27581
Orthopaedic Traumatologic Centre
L.go P.Palagi, 1 ☎ 4278227
Tuscan Orthopaedic Institute
V.le Michelangiolo, 21 ☎ 65881
Anna Meyer Hospital (for children)
V. L. Giordano, 13 ☎ 56621
General Hospital of Careggi
V.le Morgagni, 85 ☎ 4277111
San Giovanni di Dio New Hospital
Via Torregalli, 3 ☎ 71921
S. M. Annunziata Hospital
V. dell'Antella (Antella) ☎ 64490

🛪 TRAVEL AGENTS

Alijet Vacanze
V. G. Marconi, 18r ☎ 587620
Aliwest Travel
V. Paganini, 30/36 ☎ 4221201
Arno Agenzia Viaggi
P.zza Ottaviani, 7r ☎ 295251
Chiari Sommariva
B.go SS. Apostoli, 9 ☎ 295452
Cit Viaggi (S.r.l.)
V. Cavour, 56r ☎ 294307
Eyre & Humbert
V. Parione, 56r ☎ 2382251
Intertravel
V. Lamberti, 39/41r ☎ 217936
Newtours
V. G. Monaco, 20a ☎ 321155
Nobel Viaggi
B.go Ognissanti, 3r ☎ 288633
Statuto Viaggi
Piazza Muratori ☎ 470712
Universalturismo
V. degli Speziali, 7r ☎ 219873
Valtur
Via de' Vagellai, 3 ☎ 264402

⌂ HOSTELS AND CAMP SITES

Campeggio Club Firenze
V.le Guidoni, 143 ☎ 419940
Campeggio Comunale
V.le Michelangiolo, 80 ☎ 6811977
Camping Villa Camerata
V.le Righi, 2/4 ☎ 600315
Camping Panoramico Fiesole
V. Peramonda, 1 ☎ 599069
Camping Poggio degli Uccellini
V. Campagna, 38 Bivigliano ☎ 406725
Ostello della Gioventù ·
V.le Righi, 2/4 ☎ 601451
Villa Favard
V. Rocca Tedalda - Free camping site

Appartamenti Reali (Monumental)
Palazzo Pitti (by reservation only)☎ 210323

Cappella Brancacci
P.zza del Carmine ☎ 2382193
Weekdays 10am - 4.30pm
Holidays 1 - 4.30pm

Cappelle Medicee ☎ 23885
P.zza Madonna degli Aldobrandini
Open daily 9am - 2pm

Casa Buonarroti
V. Ghibellina, 70 ☎ 241752
Open daily 9.30am-1.30pm

Casa di Dante
V. S. Margherita, 1
Weekdays 9.30- 1.30pm., Holidays 9.30-12.30

Chiostri di S.M.Novella
P.zza S. M. Novella ☎ 282187
Weekdays 9am - 2pm, Holidays 8am -1pm

Galleria degli Uffizi
Loggiato degli Uffizi, 6 ☎ 23885
Weekdays 9am-7pm, Holidays 9am- 2pm

Galleria Palatina
Palazzo Pitti ☎ 2388611
Weekdays 9am - 7pm, Holidays 9am -2pm

Galleria del Costume
Palazzina della Meridiana ☎ 212557
Open daily 9am- 2pm

Galleria d'Arte Moderna
Palazzo Pitti ☎ 287096
Open daily 9am - 2pm

Galleria dell'Accademia
V. Ricasoli, 60 ☎ 23885
Weekdays 9am - 7pm; Holidays 9am -2pm

Museo e Istituto di Preistoria
V. Sant'Egidio, 21 ☎ 295159
Open daily 9.30am- 12.30pm

Museo degli Argenti (Silver Museum)
Palazzo Pitti ☎ 212557

Museo dell'Opera di Santa Croce
P.zza S. Croce, 16 ☎ 244619
Weekdays 10 -12.30pm, Holidays 3am-5pm

Museo dell'Opera del Duomo
P.zza Duomo, 9 ☎ 2302885
Open daily 9am- 7.30pm (except holidays)

Museo di Mineralogia
V. la Pira, 4 Open 9am - 1pm ☎ 2757537

Museo Ebraico di Firenze (Jewish Museum)
V. Farini, 4 (Entrance free) ☎ 245252

Museo storico "Firenze com'era"
V.dell'Oriuolo, 4 ☎ 2398483
Open daily 10am - 1pm

Museo di Storia della Fotografia
V. della Vigna Nuova, 16r ☎ 213370
Open daily 10am - 7.30pm

Museo di Storia della Scienza
P.zza dei Giudici, 1 ☎ 293493
Open daily 9.30am - 1pm

Museo di Antropologia
V. del Proconsolo, 12 ☎ 2396449
Open daily 9am - 1pm

Museo Bardini e Galleria Corsi
P.zza de' Mozzi, 1 ☎ 2342427
Weekdays 9am - 2pm, Holidays 8am-1pm

Museo Horne
V. de' Benci, 6 ☎ 244661
Weekdays 9am -1pm (closed on holidays)

Museo Nazionale del Bargello
V. del Proconsolo, 4 ☎ 23885
Open daily 9am - 2pm

Museo Archeologico
V. della Colonna, 36 ☎ 2478641
Open daily 9am - 2pm

Museo di Palazzo Davanzati
V. Porta Rossa, 13 ☎ 23885
Open daily 9am - 2pm

Museo di San Marco
P.zza San Marco, 1 ☎ 23885
Open daily 9am -2pm

Museo La Specola
V. Romana, 17 ☎ 222451
Weekdays 9am- 12pm, Holidays 9am- 1pm

Museo Marino Marini
P.zza San Pancrazio, 1 ☎ 219432
Open daily 10am - 5pm

Museo Stibbert
V. Stibbert, 26 ☎ 486049
Weekdays 9am-2pm- Holidays 9am-12.30pm

Opificio delle Pietre Dure
V. degli Alfani, 78 ☎ 294115
Open daily 9am - 1pm

Orto Botanico
V. Micheli, 3 ☎ 2757402
Open daily 9am - 12pm

Palazzo Vecchio e Quartieri Mon.
P.zza Signoria ☎ 2768465
Weekdays 9am-7pm, Holidays 8am-1pm

Raccolta "A .della Ragione" ☎ 283078
P.zza Signoria,5
Open daily 10am - 1pm

Spedale degli Innocenti
P.zza SS. Annunziata, 12 ☎ 2491708
Weekdays 8.30am- 2pm, Holidays 8.30am- 1pm

🕈 NON-CATHOLIC CHURCHES

Anglican, St. Marks
V. Maggio, 16 ☎ 294764
Sundays 9 - 10.30am
American Episcopal Church
V. Rucellai, 9 ☎ 294417
All services conducted in English
Jewish Community
V. Farini, 4 ☎ 245252
Sundays 9am- 1pm
Church of Christian Adventists
V. del Pergolino, 12 ☎ 287340
Salvation Army
V. Aretina, 91 ☎ 660445
Sundays 10.30am
Evangelical Baptist
B.go Ognissanti, 6 ☎ 210537
Sundays 11am
Evangelical Brethren
V. della Vigna Vecchia 15/17 ☎ 217236
Sundays 10.15am
Evangelical Lutheran
L.no Torrigiani, 11 ☎ 2342775
Sundays 10am
Swiss Evangelical and Reformed
L.no Torrigiani, 11 ☎ 225829
Waldensian Evangelical
V. Manzoni, 21 ☎ 2477800
Sundays 10.30am
Methodist
V. de' Benci, 9 ☎ 677462
Russian Orthodox
V. Leone X, 8 ☎ 490148
Main services 10.30am
Worship in English
Santa Maria del Fiore
Saturdays 5pm
Borgognissanti
Sundays and holidays 10am

⚑ SECOND WORLD WAR CEMETERIES

American Military Cemetery ☎ 2020020
At Falciani, about 5 miles south of Florence, on the way to Siena. Open 8am-5pm Mondays to Fridays, Saturdays 9.30am-5pm
German Military Cemetery ☎ 815248
At Traversa - Passo della Futa
Open daily 8.30am-12pm/2-7pm
British Commonwealth Military Cemetery
At Girone, 4 miles east of Florence, direc-tion Arezzo Open daily 9am-5pm
Sundays 9am-1pm
South African Cemetery of Castiglion dei Pepoli
Nearly 30 miles from Florence, on the Prato-Bologna road which crosses the Bisenzio River valley. The cemetery is 270 yards from Castiglion dei Pepoli, on the left.

💲 BANKS

Banking hours: 8.20am-1.20pm/2.45-3.45pm
Closed Saturdays and Sundays
Abbey National Bank
V. le Matteotti, 33 ☎ 5001514
Banca C. Steinhauslin
V. Sassetti, 4 ☎ 27621
Banca Commerciale Italiana
V. Strozzi, 8 ☎ 27851
Banca d'America e d'Italia
V. Strozzi, 16r ☎ 27061
Banca d'Italia
V. dell'Oriuolo, 37/39 ☎ 24931
Banca Mercantile
P.zza Davanzati, 3 ☎ 27651
Banca Naz.del Lavoro
V. dei Cerretani, 6 ☎ 23301
Banca Naz. dell'Agricoltura
V. Ricasoli, 8b ☎ 264121
Banca Naz. delle Comunicazioni
Stazione FS S.M.N. ☎ 2381470
Banca Popolare di Novara
P.zza dell'Unità Italiana, 4 ☎ 292221
Banca Toscana
V. del Corso, 6 ☎ 287018
Banco di Napoli
V. Cavour, 20/22/24 ☎ 27021
Banco di Roma
V. Vecchietti, 5
Banco di Sicilia
Piazza della Repubblica, 1a ☎ 27901
Cassa di Risparmio di Firenze
V. Bufalini, 6 ☎ 26121
Credito Italiano
V. Vecchietti, 11 ☎ 27971
Ist. Bancario S. Paolo di Torino
V. Vecchietti, 22r ☎ 27591
Ist. Mobiliare Italiano
P.zza Savonarola, 22 ☎ 579486
Monte dei Paschi di Siena
V. dei Pecori, 6/8 ☎ 49711
Nuovo Banco Ambrosiano
V. Farina, 1 ☎ 2396623

■ LIBRARIES

Biblioteca Comunale Centrale
V. Sant'Egidio, 21   ☎ 282863
Open 9am-7pm (closed on Saturdays)
Biblioteca dell'Orticoltura
V. V. Emanuele II, 4   ☎ 486743
Open 3- 7.30pm
Biblioteca "P.Thouar"
V. Mazzetta, 10   ☎ 2398740
Open 2.30 - 7.30pm
Biblioteca Mediceo-Laurenziana
P.zza San Lorenzo, 9   ☎ 210760
Open 8am - 2pm
Gabinetto "G.P. Viesseux"
Palazzo Strozzi   ☎ 288342
Open 9am-1pm - 3-7pm
Biblioteca Marucelliana
V. Cavour, 43   ☎ 216243
Open 9am - 7pm
Biblioteca Nazionale Centrale
P.zza Cavalleggeri, 1   ☎ 249191
Open 9am - 7pm

🏺 MARKETS

Mercato Centrale di S. Lorenzo
V. dell'Ariento
Straw Market
P.zza del Mercato Nuovo
Flea Market
P.zza de' Ciompi
Mercato di Santo Spirito
P.zza Santo Spirito
Mercato di Sant'Ambrogio
P.zza Lorenzo Ghiberti
Mercato delle Cascine
Parco delle Cascine

✉ POST OFFICE

Main Post Office
Palazzo delle Poste, V. Pellicceria
Information Office   ☎   160

⌂ HOTELS

☆☆☆☆☆

Excelsior
P.zza Ognissanti, 3   ☎ 294301
Grand Hotel
P.zza Ognissanti, 1   ☎ 217400
Grand Hotel Villa Medici
V. il Prato, 42   ☎ 211132
Helvetia e Bristol
V. dei Pescioni, 2   ☎ 287814
Regency Umbria
P.zza M. D'Azeglio, 3   ☎ 245247
Savoy
P.zza della Repubblica, 7 ☎283313
Villa Cora
V.le Machiavelli, 18   ☎ 2298451

☆☆☆☆

Adriatico
V. M. Finiguerra, 9   ☎ 2381781
Anglo American
V. Garibaldi, 9   ☎ 282114
Augustus
Vicolo dell'Oro, 5   ☎ 283054
Baglioni
P.zza dell'Unità Italiana, 6   ☎   23580
Bernini Palace
P.zza S. Firenze, 29   ☎ 288621
Continental
L.no Acciaiuoli, 2   ☎ 282392
De La Ville
P.zza Antinori, 1   ☎2381805
Della Signoria
V. delle Terme, 1   ☎ 214530
Executive
V. Curtatone, 5   ☎ 217451
Grand Hotel Minerva
P.zza S. M. Novella, 16   ☎ 284555
Jolly
P.zza V. Veneto, 4a   ☎   2770
Kraft
V. Solferino, 2   ☎ 284273
Lungarno
B.go San Jacopo, 14   ☎ 264211
Majestic
V. del Melarancio, 1   ☎ 264021
Starhotel Michelangelo
V.le F.lli Rosselli, 2   ☎   2784
Montebello Splendid
V. Montebello, 60   ☎ 2398051

Nord Florence		**Embassy House**	
V. F. Baracca, 199a	☎ 431151	V. Nazionale, 23	☎ 2382266
Plaza Hotel Lucchesi		**Fleming Vivahotels**	
L.no Zecca Vecchia	☎ 26236	V.le Guidoni, 87	☎ 4376773
Principe		**Gioia**	
L.no A. Vespucci, 34	☎ 284848	V. Cavour, 25	☎ 282804
Queen Palace		**Goldoni**	
V. Solferino, 5	☎ 2396818	B.go Ognissanti, 8	☎ 284080
Rivoli		**Hermitage Hotel Pension**	
V. della Scala, 33	☎ 282853	Vc. Marzio, 1	☎ 287216
Sheraton		**Il Guelfo Bianco**	
V. G. Agnelli, 33	☎ 64901	V. Cavour, 29	☎ 288330
Ville sull'Arno		**Leonardo da Vinci**	
L.no C. Colombo, 1/3/5	☎ 670971	V. G. Monaco, 12	☎ 357751

☆☆☆

		Mediterraneo	
		L.no del Tempio, 44	☎ 660241
Alba		**Porta Rossa**	
V. della Scala, 22	☎ 282610	V. Porta Rossa, 19	☎ 287551
Ambasciatori		**Privilege**	
V. L. Alamanni, 3	☎ 287421	L.no Zecca Vecchia	☎ 2341221
Arizona		**Rex**	
V. Farini, 2	☎ 245321	V. Faenza, 6	☎ 210453
Ariele		**Royal**	
V. Magenta, 11	☎ 211509	V. delle Ruote, 52	☎ 483287
Auto Park Hotel		**Villa le Rondini**	
V. Valdegola, 1	☎ 431771	V. Bologese Vecchia, 224	☎ 400081
Balestri		**Villa Liberty**	
P.zza Mentana, 7	☎ 214743	V.le Michelangelo, 40	☎ 6810581
Byron			
V. della Scala, 49	☎ 280852		

☆☆

California		**Apollo**	
V. Ricasoli, 30	☎ 282753	V. Faenza, 77	☎ 284119
Capitol Vivahotels		**Archibusieri**	
V.le Amendola, 34	☎ 2343201	P.zza del Pesce	☎ 287216
Cavour		**Beatrice**	
V. del Proconsolo, 3	☎ 282461	V. Fiume, 11	☎ 2396137
City		**Casci**	
V. S. Antonino, 18	☎ 211543	V. Cavour, 13	☎ 211686
Classic		**Crocini**	
V.le Machiavelli, 25	☎ 229351	C.so Italia, 38	☎ 210171
Columbus		**Derby**	
L.no C. Colombo, 22a	☎ 677251	V. Nazionale, 35	☎ 219308
Cristallo		**Giselda**	
V. Cavour, 27	☎ 215375	V. L. Alamanni, 5	☎ 284617
Dante		**Kursaal**	
V. S. Cristofano, 2	☎ 241772	V. Nazionale, 24	☎ 496324
David		**La Pergola**	
V.le Michelangelo, 1	☎ 6811695	V. A delPollaiolo, 16	☎ 700896
De La Pace		**Nizza**	
V. Lamarmora, 28	☎ 577343	V. del Giglio, 5	☎ 2396897
Duomo		**Orcagna**	
P.zza Duomo, 1	☎ 219922	V. Orcagna, 57	☎ 669959

Acqua al 2
V. della Vigna Vecchia, 40r ☎ 284170
Acquerello
V. Ghibellina, 156r ☎ 2340554
Al Lume di Candela
V. delle Terme, 23r ☎ 294566
Alfredo
V.le G. Don Minzoni, 3r ☎ 578291
Alfredo sull'Arno
V. dei Bardi, 46r ☎ 283808
Alle Murate
V. Ghibellina, 52r ☎ 240618
Antico Crespino
L.go E. Fermi, 14 ☎ 221155
Baccus
B.go Ognissanti, 45r ☎ 283714
Beatrice
V. del Proconsolo, 31r ☎ 2398123
Buca Mario
P.zza Ottaviani, 16r ☎ 214179
Cammillo
B.go S. Jacopo, 57r ☎ 212427
Cantinetta Antinori
P.zza Antinori, 3 ☎ 292234
Celestino
P.zza S. Felicita, 4r ☎ 2396574
Coco Lezzone
V. del Parioncino, 26r ☎ 287178
Dino
V. Ghibellina, 51r ☎ 241452
Don Chisciotte
V. C. Ridolfi, 4/6r ☎ 475430
Enoteca Pinchiorri
V. Ghibellina, 87 ☎ 242777
Harry's Bar
L.no A. Vespucci, 22r ☎ 2396700
Il Bargello
P.zza Signoria, 4r ☎ 214071
Il Cibreo
V. de' Macci, 118r ☎ 2341100
Il Fagiano
V. de' Neri, 57r ☎ 287876
Il Latini
V. dei Palchetti, 6r ☎ 210916
La Loggia
P.le Michelangelo, 1 ☎ 2342832
Le Rampe
V.le G. Poggi ☎ 6811891
Oliviero
V. delle Terme, 51r ☎ 212421

Il Barone di Porta Romana
V. Romana, 123r ☎ 220585
Osteria N° 1
V. del Moro, 22 ☎ 284897
Pepolino
V. C. F. Ferrucci, 16r ☎ 608905
Pallottino
V. Isola delle Stinche, 1r ☎ 289573
Perseus
V.le Don Minzoni, 10r ☎ 588226
Sabatini
V. Panzani, 9a ☎ 211559
Taverna del Bronzino
V. delle Ruote, 25r ☎ 495220
Vecchia Firenze
B.go degli Albizi, 18 ☎ 2340361

🍴 TRATTORIE

Angiolino
V. S. Spirito, 36r ☎ 2398976
Antica Mescita San Niccolò
V. S. Niccolò, 60r ☎ 2342836
Belle Donne
V. delle Belle Donne, 16r ☎ 2382609
Bibe
V. delle Bagnese, 1r ☎ 2049085
Il Lorenzaccio
P.zza della Signoria, 34r ☎ 294553
La Baraonda
V. Ghibellina, 67r ☎ 2341171
La Beppa di Ricci & C.
V. dell'Erta Canina, 6r ☎ 2342742
Mastro Bulletta
V. Cento Stelle, 27r ☎ 571275
Palle D'Oro
V. Sant'Antonino, 43/45r ☎ 288383

⌁ CHINESE RESTAURANTS

China Town
V. Vecchietti, 6/8/10r   ☎ 294470
Fior di Loto
V. dei Servi, 35r   ☎ 2398235
Il Mandarino
V. Condotta, 17r   ☎ 2396130
Nuova Cina
P.zza S. M. Novella, 9/10/11   ☎ 215387
Peking
V. del Melarancio, 21r   ☎ 282922

♫ FLORENCE BY NIGHT

Discos

Full-up
V. della Vigna Vecchia, 21r   ☎ 293006
Jackie O'
V. dell'Erta Canina, 24a   ☎ 2342442
Kasar
L.no Colombo, 17   ☎ 666962
Meccanò Meccanò
V. degli Olmi, 1   ☎ 331371
Space Electronic
V. Palazzuolo, 37   ☎ 293082

═▼ PIZZAS AND SANDWICHES

Borgo Antico
P.zza S. Spirito, 6r   ☎ 210437
Danny Rock
V. Pandolfini, 13r   ☎ 2340307
Dante
P.zza N.Sauro, 12r   ☎ 293215
Edy House
P.zza Savonarola, 9r   ☎ 588886
Hydra
V. Canto dei Nelli, 38r   ☎ 218922
Il Crostino
V. Borghini, 9r   ☎ 5001869
Italy & Italy
P.zza Stazione, 25r   ☎ 282885
Nuti
B.go S. Lorenzo, 39r   ☎ 210145
Yellow Bar
V. del Proconsolo, 39r   ☎ 211766

☕ CAFÉS

Gilli
P.zza della Repubblica, 39r   ☎ 2396310
Giubbe Rosse
P.zza della Repubblica, 13/14r   ☎ 212280
Paszkowsky
P.zza della Repubblica, 6r   ☎ 210236
Rivoire
P.zza Signoria, 5r   ☎ 211302

ⓨ PIANO BARS AND NIGHT CLUBS

Apollo Bar
V. dell' Ariento, 41r   ☎ 219751
Cabiria Café
P.zza S. Spirito, 4r   ☎ 215732
Dolce Vita
P.zza del Carmine, 6r   ☎ 284595
Montecarla Club
V. dei Bardi, 2   ☎ 2340259
Il Rifrullo
V. San Niccolò, 53/57   ☎ 342621
Porfirio Rubirosa
V.le Strozzi, 38r   ☎ 490965
Rose's
V. del Parione, 26r   ☎ 287090

🎥 CINEMAS and THEATRES

Ariston - P.zza Ottaviani, 3r
Astra - V. Cerretani, 54r
Capitol - V. Castellani, 36r
Excelsior - V. Cerretani, 4r
Gambrinus - V. Brunelleschi, 1
Odeon - V. Sassetti, 1
Teatro Comunale - C.so Italia, 20
Teatro Comunale - V. Solferino, 15
Teatro della Pergola - V. Pergola, 12
Teatro Niccolini - V. Ricasoli, 5
Teatro Verdi - V. Ghibellina, 99

Revised Edition April 2001

© Copyright 1999 by Bonechi Edizioni "Il Turismo" S.r.l
Via dei Rustici, 5 - 50122 Florence
Tel. +39 (055) 239.82.24/25 - Fax +39 (055) 21.63.66
E-mail address: barbara@bonechi.com
                bbonechi@dada.it
http://www.bonechi.com
Printed in Italy
All rights reserved

Cover and Pagination: Claudia Baggiani
Text Revision: Lorena Lazzari
Drawing on page 91: Ombretta Dinelli and Marco Nestucci
Black and white drawings: Patrick Hamilton
Photography: Archives of Bonechi Edizioni "Il Turismo" S.r.l.
Stampa: BO.BA.DO.MA, Florence
ISBN 88-7204-289-5

We wish to thank Ombretta Dinelli and Marco Nestucci, architects,
for their complimentary permission to print the photograph on page 91.